America, Welcome to
the Poorhouse

America, Welcome to the Poorhouse

WHAT YOU MUST DO TO PROTECT YOUR FINANCIAL FUTURE AND THE REFORM WE NEED

JANE WHITE

Vice President, Publisher: Tim Moore
Associate Publisher and Director of Marketing: Amy Neidlinger
Executive Editor: Jim Boyd
Editorial Assistant: Pamela Boland
Development Editor: Russ Hall
Operations Manager: Gina Kanouse
Digital Marketing Manager: Julie Phifer
Publicity Manager: Laura Czaja
Assistant Marketing Manager: Megan Colvin
Cover Designer: Alan Clements
Managing Editor: Kristy Hart
Project Editor: Lori Lyons
Copy Editor: Cheri Clark
Proofreader: Kay Hoskin
Indexer: Angela Martin
Compositor: Jake McFarland
Manufacturing Buyer: Dan Uhrig

© 2010 by Jane White

Publishing as FT Press

Upper Saddle River, New Jersey 07458

This book is sold with the understanding that neither the author nor the publisher is engaged in rendering legal, accounting, or other professional services or advice by publishing this book. Each individual situation is unique. Thus, if legal or financial advice or other expert assistance is required in a specific situation, the services of a competent professional should be sought to ensure that the situation has been evaluated carefully and appropriately. The author and the publisher disclaim any liability, loss, or risk resulting directly or indirectly, from the use or application of any of the contents of this book.

FT Press offers excellent discounts on this book when ordered in quantity for bulk purchases or special sales. For more information, please contact U.S. Corporate and Government Sales, 1-800-382-3419, corpsales@pearsontechgroup.com. For sales outside the U.S., please contact International Sales at international@pearson.com.

Company and product names mentioned herein are the trademarks or registered trademarks of their respective owners.

Printed in the United States of America

First Printing September 2009

ISBN-10: 0-13-702017-1
ISBN-13: 978-0-13-702017-1

Pearson Education LTD.
Pearson Education Australia PTY, Limited.
Pearson Education Singapore, Pte. Ltd.
Pearson Education North Asia, Ltd.
Pearson Education Canada, Ltd.
Pearson Educación de Mexico, S.A. de C.V.
Pearson Education—Japan
Pearson Education Malaysia, Pte. Ltd.

Library of Congress Cataloging-in-Publication Data

White, Jane, 1948-
   America, welcome to the poorhouse : what you must do to protect your financial future and the reform we need / Jane White.
      p. cm.
   ISBN 978-0-13-702017-1 (hbk. : alk. paper) 1. Retirement income—United States—Planning.
2. Finance, Personal—United States. 3. Finance—Government policy—United States. I. Title.
   HG179.W5229 2009
   332.02400973—dc22

                           2009023705

Contents

Acknowledgments

When you write a book, you're "dependent on the kindness of strangers"—or people who know you and don't mind lending a hand.

I couldn't have written this book without the input of the following people, in alphabetical order: Ginna Green, Keith Gumbinger, Bill Karbon, Judy Kennedy, Fred Reish, Massie Rich, Luke Swarthout, and James Turpin. Thanks to Mark Zandi from Moody's Economy.com for access to his great research. And last, but definitely not least, thanks to Jim Boyd for being a great editor.

About the Author

Jane White is Founder and President of Retirement Solutions, LLC, which promotes 401(k) reform and provides investment education. In 2007, at the U.S. Department of Labor's invitation, White presented recommended 401(k) contribution rates to the ERISA Advisory Council. As a result of White's testimony, the Working Group on Financial Literacy recommended that the DOL "encourage plan communication that uses income replacement formulas and final pay multiples." A Congressionally appointed delegate to the 2002 National Summit on Retirement Savings, White first observed the 401(k) savings crisis in 1993 as associate editor of Standard & Poor's Your Financial Future, distributed to a half a million 401(k) participants. A former syndicated personal finance columnist for Gannett News Service, White first observed the housing bubble and the risk of adjustable rate mortgages in her 1991 book, *The Cost Conscious Homebuyer's Guide*. Her articles have appeared in *The New York Times, Barron's, and Employee Benefit News*.

Are You Better Off Than You Were as a Kid?

The nationally broadcast debate in 1980 between President Jimmy Carter and would-be President Ronald Reagan was summed up in 10 short words: "Are you better off than you were four years ago?"

For Carter, the situation was dire. Iranian radicals had held 52 American hostages for nearly a year. The economy had nose-dived while inflation skyrocketed. Nothing Carter said could counter Reagan's rhetorical question. It was Reagan's debate and a week later it was Reagan's election.

Today if you ask yourself, "Am I better off than I was growing up?" the answer may very well be no. This time it's not a war or hyper-inflation that's threatening America (although we're still paying through the nose for gasoline prices), but financial stress.

Despite the fact that many Americans may appear to be wealthy, too many have been "living on leverage"—over their heads in debt—unless they've got "chief" and "officer" in their job titles because most of what they own is paid for with borrowed money—whether it's credit card debt or home equity loans—not with rising wages. While in 1980 the average CEO wage was 42 times that of the average worker, in 2008 it was 208 times, averaging $7.7 million. At the same time, the average weekly earnings for Americans has actually decreased in the past 30 years, from more than $325 in the early 1970s to about $280 in 2005 (in 1982 dollars).

In March of 2009 a poll by CNN Opinion Research Corp. showed that only 39% of respondents thought they'd be able to keep up their quality of life—down from 45% the previous year. Only 50%

of homeowners said they were very confident they could keep making mortgage payments, down from 58% a year earlier. Only 24% of parents said they were very confident they'd be able to afford to send their children to college. And only 22% of working people thought they'd be able to save enough for retirement.

The Four Biggest Sources of Financial Stress: Empty Nest Eggs, Unaffordable Homes, Overpriced Colleges, Credit Card Debt

What's tragic is that outside of CNN's reference to pension stress, the biggest financial crisis that the media isn't covering is that most of us will be pensionless or pension-poor when we stop working—if we can afford to. From 1974 to 2004, the percentage of Americans covered by a defined benefit plan shrank from 44% of the workforce to 17%, according to the Employee Benefit Research Institute. At the same time, more than 80% of the private-sector workforce is employed by a company that only offers a 401(k) plan, in which you pretty much have to bankroll your own pension—because the U.S. employer contribution rate is the second lowest in the world. Bottom line: With few exceptions, nobody can retire if they have only a 401(k) plan. The you-know-what will hit the fan in 2011 when the first wave of Baby Boomers is scheduled to retire and can't afford to.

I first observed the 401(k) crisis in 1993 shortly after landing a job as associate editor of a newsletter distributed to half a million 401(k) participants with their quarterly statements. While as a financial writer I had covered topics such as mortgages and the stock market, I wasn't very familiar with 401(k) plans—and at that point, there wasn't much media coverage of them—it wasn't until the Enron collapse that the term "401(k)" was coin of the realm.

Although most Americans participate in these plans, the plans' names will vary with the employer.

Once I started digging, I was alarmed to find out that, unlike a traditional pension, in which the employer traditionally invests enough money that employees can replace 70% of their salaries until they die—assuming that they have worked for the company long enough to be "vested" in the plan—401(k) accounts have no such promises.

While there was some panic about 401(k) plans being risky in late 2008, the focus on the stock market slump was off-base. The problem with 401(k) plans isn't that their investments are too risky, it's that the cost of funding employee accounts is left largely up to the employees. Not only do many employers get away with not contributing a dime to their employees' accounts, but when they do at best it's typically only a matching contribution of 50 cents for every dollar you put in, or equivalent to 3% of your pay. This contribution rate is the second lowest in the world—even Mexico's is higher, at 6% of pay.

The second source of financial stress for 50% or more of Americans is overpriced housing. When it comes to housing, we have two problems: an overpriced market whose bubble has burst and irresponsible lending practices that have yet to be reined in. Although the median home price was a little more than three times the median wage in 1976, a mere five years later it was more than four times the median wage and it's currently six times the median wage.

In 2008, as the housing bubble was bursting, not since the Depression had a larger share of Americans owed more on their homes than they were worth—often referred to as being "under water." Nearly 8.8 million homeowners, or more than 10% of the total, were under water in 2008, more than double the number in 2007. Although the housing slumps of the mid-1970s and late 1980s were confined to the coasts, the recent bust has cut a far wider path and has come at a time when home debt was at its highest level since World War II.

Why do we care about overpriced homes? Because a house isn't just a roof over your head, it's the fourth leg of the "four-legged chair" that makes up your retirement equity—along with pensions (if you're lucky enough to have one), Social Security, and 401(k) savings. One reason the "Greatest Generation" could retire comfortably is that many of them had pensions *and* most of them stayed in their homes for most of their careers—in other words, they had a "buy-and-hold" home investment strategy as opposed to trading up to homes that they couldn't afford, as is the case with many people today.

Many would-be homeowners who are living in areas where homes are overpriced and unaffordable may have to face the initially daunting prospect of moving to regions where homes are affordable *and* jobs are plentiful. What's more, those of you who are living in depressed areas in Michigan and Ohio may need to consider the same thing, for precisely the opposite reason: It's not affordability that's the issue but the risk that your home will be worth less than what you paid for it when you retire because your local economy has tanked.

The third source of financial stress is that college costs have skyrocketed at a time when the majority of Americans need a college education to succeed in a globalized world. With so many service and factory jobs being outsourced to India and China, we've got to aim for the majority of the next generation to get a college degree. The good news is that this crucial need is on President Barack Obama's radar screen: In an address to a Joint Session of Congress in late February of 2009, he said, "I ask every American to commit to at least one year or more of higher education or career training. This can be community college or a four-year school; vocational training or an apprenticeship. But whatever the training may be, every American will need to get more than a high-school diploma."

Finally, credit card debt and home equity loans have enabled us to live beyond our means—at the same time forcing us to pay many times the sticker price of an item because of the corrosive influence of compound interest in reverse—at a point when we need all the extra money we can get to save for retirement and pay for our kids' college education.

This book is organized in order of "financial stress levels": Retirement comes first because at least 80% of the population can't afford to retire, mortgages are second because half of the population is under mortgage stress, college costs come third because most people need a college degree to succeed in a world where we're competing against low-wage labor abroad, and credit card debt is fourth because 35 million people pay only the minimum balance on their bills, increasing the cost of the debt.

In each section, I'll look at the cause of the financial stress, propose legislative reforms to solve the problems, offer advice on how you can manage your finances until we get reform, and suggest an action plan to get reform. In a nutshell, reform means tripling the employer 401(k) contribution rate to equal 9% of pay as is the case in Australia, outlawing adjustable rate mortgages, lowering the cost of college, and cutting down on credit card debt and home equity loans.

Why do we need reform when we've got a reform-minded President in the White House? Because there's only so much President Obama can do when too many members of Congress and the Senate are compromised by campaign contributions from the business lobby.

The first reason we need to shut down K Street, the location in Washington where most lobbyists have their offices, is because of the influence that the business lobby has on politics. There are now 15,000 lobbyists in Washington—27 for every member of Congress. The second reason is that there's no law against a politician becoming a lobbyist—there's only a "cooling-off period" between the time the politician works for taxpayers and the time he or she works for lobbyists—which means these politicians are often likely to draft or change language to make legislation more business-friendly, versus taxpayer-friendly. According to Public Citizen, a consumer advocacy organization, between 1998 and 2004, some 42% of former House members and 50% of former senators who were available to do so became registered lobbyists.

The good news is that the internet has unleashed a revolution in fundraising, campaigning, and communicating. In the same fashion that small contributions from millions of voters—along with leverage from king-makers like Oprah Winfrey—catapulted Barack Obama from a long shot to a front-runner, the virtual grass-roots movement can ensure that Congress and President Obama continue to work for the electorate.

The better news is that we've got a new administration in the White House. President Obama has set up a Middle Class Task Force that promises to reach out to Americans and address the causes of their financial stress, from healthcare coverage to pension security. I'm hoping that my readers can convince him to aim for boosting Americans' wealth so that more of them stay or move into the upper middle class.

It's time for a second American Revolution.

PART I

80% of Americans Can't Afford to Retire

Chapter 1

Why You Can't Retire from a 401(k) Plan: You Won't Have Ten Times Your Salary in Your Account at Age 65

Mention the word *Australia* and the images that come to mind are "shrimps on the barbie," koala bears, and kangaroos. I'd like to add another image: people who can actually afford to retire.

A report issued in January 2008 by AMP Financial Services, a firm that manages Australian retirement funds and also reports on retirement readiness, revealed that Australians between the ages of 30 and 34 are projected to have assets of more than $540,000 in today's dollars in their accounts by the time they are ready to retire; those between 20 and 24 will have nearly $700,000.

How do those six-digit projected nest eggs for the typical Australian compare with the nest egg of a typical American approaching retirement? Unlike its Australian counterpart, the Investment Company Institute (ICI), the U.S. trade group for mutual funds, doesn't measure whether 401(k) participants are on track, only whether assets have grown. In 2007, the ICI issued a news release reporting that Americans held $2.75 trillion in 401(k) plans. While ICI President Paul Schott Stevens was quoted as saying, "Ensuring that working Americans are preparing for retirement is a public policy of vital concern," nowhere in its report is it stated whether this amount divided by 52.2 million 401(k) participants equals an adequate nest egg.

Here's the bad news: According to Fidelity Investments' 2007 report on its clients, the median balance for workers on the cusp of retirement, age 60 to 65, was a measly $43,000—not enough to last most people a year or so—and that would apply only to people earning $43,000 in that age group. The formula that's often used by pension actuaries to calculate a benefit is ten times "final pay"—or the salary you're earning right before retirement. If most 65-year-olds have only around $43,000, they won't be able to afford to retire for another decade or more—higher earners are in an even worse predicament.

Australian Employers Must Contribute the Equivalent of 9% of Pay and Can't "Suspend" Contributions to Employee Accounts

The reason Australians' nest eggs are fuller than those of their American counterparts? Very simply, Australian employers are required to contribute to workers' superannuation (Australia's word for pension) accounts—the current contribution rate is the equivalent of 9% of salary—three times the typical U.S. employer contribution rate—up to a salary ceiling of $137,880 up to age 75. In addition, the contribution is made regardless of whether the employee contributes—it's not simply a "matching contribution." One in four Americans doesn't contribute to a 401(k) account and therefore ends up with nothing.

What's more, Australian employers aren't allowed to stop or "suspend" making contributions when the economy sags, as is the case in the U.S. More than 60 major U.S. employers announced that they were lowering or suspending contributions in the U.S. as of early 2009, including *Reader's Digest*, Sprint Nextel, U.S. Steel, Unisys, FedEx, and Eastman Kodak.

Australians Can Sell Homes to Boost Their Retirement Accounts

While contribution limits for American workers over age 50 are capped at $22,000 in 2009 (indexed to inflation), Baby Boomer Australians can sell a home or another asset and add the proceeds to their accounts. Under changes introduced in the 2006 budget, workers over age 60 can make after-tax superannuation contributions of $150,000 a year, or $450,000 over three years. Unlike their American counterparts, the Australian government realizes that Boomers need this brute-force opportunity to jump-start their savings because the 9% guarantee was only instituted in 2002—with the result that Boomer Australians will benefit from fewer years of super contributions than their Gen X or Gen Y counterparts.

The result of this stewardship? Australians actually contributed more to their accounts than their employers did in the second quarter of 2007; according to the Australian Prudential Regulation Authority, employees contributed $22.4 billion, compared to $18.9 billion by employers on their behalf.

Other Countries Are Pension-Richer

Australia's pension system isn't the only one that's putting ours to shame. According to a report by the Organization for Economic Cooperation and Development, the United States ranks near the bottom of the 30 member countries in pension generosity. Only six of the member countries had lower pension wealth than the U.S.

Australia is one of eight countries that has a mandatory 401(k) style system and six of them are more generous than ours; the average employer contribution rate is equal to 7.25% of pay. Denmark's is equal to 11.8%, Hungary's is 8%, Mexico's is 6.5%, Poland's is 7.3%, the Slovak Republic's is 9%, and Sweden's is 4.5%.

CEO Pay Is 208 Times the Average Joe's, Whose Wages Are Shrinking

Not only do much of the rest of the world's pension systems put ours to shame, but pension poverty for the middle class is occurring at a point when the "CEO class" is taking home sky-high paychecks. In 1980, the average CEO wage was 42 times that of the ordinary worker. As of 2008 it was 208 times—averaging $7.7 million. At the same time, the average weekly earnings for Americans has actually decreased in the past three decades, from more than $325 in the early 1970s to about $280 in 2005 (in 1982 dollars).

If the median wage had increased at the same rate as that of the top brass since 1980, it would be $79,000 instead of the current median wage of about $37,000. With that kind of salary, many more middle-class Americans would be able to afford a bigger chunk of their kids' college bills rather than needing loans to pay for most of them. More of them could afford to put 20% down on a home purchase and therefore avoid taking out risky adjustable-rate mortgages. They could even afford to contribute more to their 401(k) accounts, perhaps closer to the 12.6% of pay contributed by Australians versus about 5% for Americans.

If anything, it's the increasing productivity of the average American worker that is boosting America's bottom line. According to Mercer Human Resource Consulting, while corporate profits rose 15% a year from 2002 to 2005 and CEO compensation rose by an average of 7.2% per year, wages of exempt employees rose by an average of 1.1% per year—which instead of a raise is actually a "lower" if you factor in yearly inflation rates of about 3%.

How Good Times, Bad Times, and "Pension Reform" Took a Wrecking Ball to Our Pension System

Before we look at how you can make the most of your 401(k) plan and offer strategies for getting Congress to pass my proposed 401(k) Security Act, which would mandate 9% employer contributions, it's worth it to learn how our pension system went astray.

If you grew up in the 1950s through the early 1970s, there was a good chance that your dad was covered by a regular pension, also known as a defined benefit plan, because the economy was booming, unions had more clout, and employers needed to offer perks to lure employees. (I'm saying *dad* and not *mom* because in those days it was rare for moms to work outside the home.) However, starting in the 1970s, companies started cutting back on pensions, as "stagflation" and increased competition from Japanese manufacturers threw our economy into a tailspin.

From 1974 to 2004, the percentage of Americans covered by a defined benefit plan shrank from 44% of the workforce to 17% of it, according to the Employee Benefit Research Institute. At the same time, more than 60% of the workforce is employed by a company that offers only a 401(k) plan. What's remarkable about this downward trend is that while the law that governs pensions, the Employee Retirement Income Security Act (ERISA), has been amended at least 40 times in the past 30 years, the result is fewer pensions, not more or better pensions.

In fact, during the nine months after ERISA was signed into law, the Pension Benefit Guarantee Corporation, the agency that insures pensions, was socked with 5,000 terminations (plans that were ended), a result that has not registered on the minds of members of Congress or the general public, since few in the media have covered this trend. At the same time, in the following three decades, employers proceeded to raid and shut down pensions when times were good and terminate them when times were bad.

Remember the 1980s? The images that come to mind aren't just bad fashion and big-lens glasses, but also corporate greed—remember Gordon Gekko? High interest rates earned on pension investments created "surpluses" that the companies could use to acquire other companies. The companies would simply terminate the pensions and pay out the smaller pension in the form of an annuity. At the same time, corporate raiders targeted companies with "overfunded" plans, using the surpluses to pay off debt associated with their leveraged buyouts. Congress put an end to this practice in 1990 by imposing a 50% excise tax on reclaimed surpluses. (Needless to say, in a logical world there would be tolerance for the concept of overfunding, since this so-called surplus is needed to bolster balances when the stock market is heading south.)

On the other hand, the bear market during the first eight years of this century was also damaging for defined benefit plans. With stocks plunging and the Fed cutting interest rates, many companies were forced to kick in substantial amounts of cash. While employer contributions to pension plans averaged about $30 billion a year from 1980 to 2000, during 2002 and 2003 companies had to kick in close to $100 billion annually.

In the same fashion that the creation of ERISA caused the death of the very pensions it was intended to protect, the so-called Pension Protection Act of 2006, which makes funding requirements more costly, may protect pensions for some but will shrink them for many others. Roughly 20% to 25% of the nation's $2.3 trillion of assets in defined benefit plans have recently been frozen—meaning that some or all of the employees stop earning benefits, and others who are new hires won't have any coverage.

Too Many Rules + Voluntary Pension Plans = Dead Plans

The problem with putting too many rules on a voluntary scheme is that employers react by dropping out of the scheme. As Thomas Donlan of *Barron's* put it, "The new pension law will drive companies in financial stress to put their pension plans into the care of the government insurance agency. At the same time, it will drive prosperous companies to take their retirement plans out of the defined benefit system." In 2007, more than 1,200 employers ended their pension plans, according to the Pension Benefit Guarantee Corporation.

ERISA: Simultaneously Complex and Useless

Former Secretary of Labor Robert Reich called ERISA the "single most complicated piece of legislation ever to be enacted, subsequently providing guaranteed livelihoods to thousands of lawyers and administrators"—detractors have nicknamed it "Every Rotten Idea Since Adam." The irony about 401(k) plans is that although ERISA has strict requirements for the "fiduciaries" of the plan, the people responsible for overseeing the investments—which include acting solely in the interest of plan participants, diversifying plan investments, and charging only reasonable expenses, there is no requirement to carry out the most prudent practice of all, which is to tell people how much to contribute to their accounts.

Although 401(k) plans are also called defined contribution plans, to my knowledge no elected representative has ever attempted to amend ERISA to require that the necessary contributions be defined so that the participant can retire with a benefit as generous as that of a defined benefit plan. While the Pension Protection Act provided clarification on the ability of 401(k) advisers to tell participants which funds to invest in, it provided no guidance on advising the participants on their required contribution rate based on how much they've already saved and their "investment time horizon," that is, how many years they are away from retirement—communication that is vastly more vital to help participants achieve retirement readiness than advice on which funds to invest in.

While the Department of Labor is constantly issuing guidance and regulations about investment advice—the latest is allowing participants to get advice by a "computer model certified as unbiased and through a fiduciary adviser compensated on a level fee basis,"—there is no component of the advice feature that deals with how much you need to contribute. What's more, nobody should have to pay a human being for this advice. Participants should be able to buy software that essentially gives the same advice to everybody, which is to contribute the maximum, don't time the market, and stick with index funds—advice that I'll detail in the next chapter. (Disclosure: I'm interested in developing this software.)

Finally, investment advice that takes place at the workplace flies in the face of common sense: If the typical American changes jobs an average of every four years, most of their 401(k) assets are often in rollover IRAs or at previous employers, not in their current 401(k) accounts.

Why Has There Been No Retirement Reform? Most So-Called Experts Are Clueless About What's Needed to Make 401(k) Plans Walk, Talk, and Quack Like a Pension

In reality, the 401(k) plan is an "accidental pension." The IRS code that spawned the 401(k) plan was meant to clear up a dispute over the taxation of profit-sharing plans, not to create retirement security. According to Ted Benna, the consultant who "invented" the 401(k) plan in 1980, his idea was to redesign a retirement program to capitalize on tax breaks and add security to an existing defined benefit plan—not to replace it.

The problem is that very few people who advise 401(k) plans or sponsor the plans seem to know the formula for making a 401(k) account adequate enough to replace a defined benefit pension. One exception is David Wray, the president of the Profit-Sharing/401k Council of America, a group of 1,200 employers, who was quoted in the *Seattle Times* in 2005 as saying that 401(k) participants need to aim to have the equivalent of ten times their final pay in their accounts. "Ten times final pay gets it done," Wray said. "The issue is the 40 years. You've got to start at 25 to retire at 65."

Wray hit the nail on the head. Or if 401(k) participants haven't started contributing to their accounts at age 25 and are contributing less than 10% of their salaries to their accounts, they've got to goose up their contributions—even higher if they've waited until age 35, 45, or 55, as I'll explain a little later.

Incredibly, at the time this book was going to print, if you Google the phrase "ten times final pay," you'll only get nine results. Why is this phrase no longer coin of the realm? That's because the pension actuaries who used to be hired by employers to make sure they followed ERISA's rules for funding pensions aren't required to play this role when it comes to 401(k) plans. Since there are no rules for funding 401(k) plans, pretty much the only role pension actuaries play is to help employers follow other ERISA rules pertaining to 401(k) plans, such as "nondiscrimination" testing and other counterintuitive rules that prevent highly paid people from contributing enough to their accounts so that they can retire.

My Testimony Before the U.S. Department of Labor on Recommended Disclosure of Required Contribution Rates

Until we get genuine 401(k) reform, at a minimum, 401(k) participants have the right to know how much to contribute to their accounts—their "co-pay" if you will—to fund a nest egg that will equal ten times their final pay at retirement. With the input of pension actuary James E. Turpin of the Turpin Consulting Group, I developed formulas for contribution rates required based on the current typical employer match of 3%. I was invited to present these findings as a witness before the Department of Labor's (DOL) 2007 ERISA Advisory Council's Working Group on Financial Literacy and the Role of the

Employer. As a result, the Working Group ultimately recommended to the DOL that employees should be told how much they need to contribute to achieve a multiple of their salary nearing retirement. Unfortunately, even if the DOL agreed that this communication was necessary, its recommendations aren't laws that employers have to follow.

What was disclosed in my testimony is that the most important advice that 401(k) participants need isn't which investments to pick but the percentage of their salary they need to sock away depending on their investment time horizon. In other words, the earlier you start saving, the smaller the percentage of income you have to set aside—and vice versa.

Also, assuming a typical employer contribution rate of 3% of pay, even the tiny minority of participants who are savvy enough to start contributing at age 25 must save 10% of their salary to build an adequate nest egg by age 65. The longer the participant postpones starting to contribute, the greater the required contribution. For example:

- Waiting until age 35 increases the contribution rate to more than 17%.
- Waiting until age 40 increases it to more than 23% of pay.
- Finally, waiting until age 50 requires nearly a five-fold increase from the rate at age 25, to 48% of pay. Needless to say, this over-50 requirement flies in the face of the meager current $5,500 limit on "catch-up contributions" currently allowed by the IRS.

Mutual Fund Companies Are Unaware Their Clients Can't Retire

Unfortunately, few pension advocates appear to have consulted pension actuaries to figure out what's needed—and therefore they don't appear to know how far behind most Americans are. Nor to my knowledge, have any mutual fund executives lobbied Congress to make 401(k) plans work—this is particularly outrageous because they are stewards of 401(k) participant assets—especially since reform would mean they'd have more assets under management. Nor has anyone proposed mandating that employers contribute more to each account so that the "co-pay" required by the participant isn't unaffordable for those who have waited until their 30s or later to start contributing—that is, most of us.

In a November 2006 *Wall Street Journal* article titled "As the 401(k) Turns 25, Has It Improved with Age?" a spokeswoman for the Investment Company Institute offered the oblique assessment that "the 401(k) is hitting its stride" without offering evidence that participants are on track to achieve an account balance equal to ten times their final pay.

In addition, while several of the large mutual fund companies produce annual reports on the 401(k) assets under management with detailed statistics on account balances, asset allocation, loans, and withdrawals, I'm unaware of any report on whether their clients are on track to reach a nest egg goal of ten times final pay—or any goal. And while many of them have launched "target date" mutual funds that gradually shift the asset allocation of the participants' accounts from stocks into bonds or cash equivalents as the participant gets closer to retirement, there is no advice to investors on the contribution rate needed to meet that target, nor is the target ever defined.

In a rare departure, Fidelity Investments issued somewhat of an alarm, albeit one that you had to dig hard to find, in its November

2007 report on corporate defined contribution plans. In the report, Fidelity introduced a "new measure of retirement readiness" called the Retirement Income Indicator, which "measures employees' progress toward accumulating sufficient workplace savings to replace at least 40% of their preretirement income." Why such a low replacement ratio? Because Fidelity assumes that participants can count on other sources of income such as a rollover IRA and/or a defined benefit pension for the rest of the income stream. Fidelity should know better, especially when it comes to the topic of shrinking defined benefit pension coverage, given that Fidelity froze the pension plan covering its 32,000 employees in March of 2007.

At least Fidelity attempts to use a measure of retirement readiness and acknowledges that a portion of its participants face bleak financial futures. In contrast, the Vanguard Group's 2007 "How America Saves" report describes 401(k) plans as "broadly successful in encouraging millions of employees to save for their retirement." What's more, it depicts enrolling employees in the plan as putting the participant "squarely on the path for success: plan participation, regular savings increases and a balanced investment program."

Nor do mutual fund managers appear to know what contribution rate is necessary for 401(k) participants—or the fact that the rate increases the later the participant starts to save. According to T. Rowe Price's 2005 report on its clients, "Some financial experts recommend that employees save 10% to 20% of their salaries each year." Gee, T. Rowe—aren't you supposed to be financial experts?

A lack of knowledge by the mutual fund industry about how much participants need to save and what size nest egg they should aim for based on their salary near retirement is evident by the flawed assumptions offered by at least two of the mutual funds in their online calculators. At the time of this writing, Vanguard instructs its users to "estimate the percent of your *current* [italics mine] income you'll need to maintain a comfortable lifestyle in retirement," as if it didn't matter whether the user was 20 or 50 years old. On the page on Fidelity's website titled, "Are You Saving Enough?," it tells users to determine how much they need based on how much they've currently saved and when they are going to retire, not their projected salary at retirement.

Media Is Unaware of Retirement Crisis

Perhaps the most frustrating obstacle to progress is the lack of media interest in the crisis. Despite sending out press releases half a dozen times a year for two years, the only publication I could convince to address the problem is the *Employee Benefit News*, for which I used to write a column.

At a forum sponsored by the Employee Benefit Research Institute in 2004 on the decline of defined benefit plans, journalist Michael Clowes, then of Crain's *Pensions & Investments*, suggested that the media won't provide much coverage of this crisis. "I think the general press has missed the overall direction of the impending demise of the corporate defined benefit plans and its implications," Clowes said. "What's more, if the media does cover 401(k) plans it will happen during a bull market and focus on the excitement of having a 401(k) plan."

Clowes *almost* hit the nail on the head, but perhaps even he didn't realize that having a 401(k) account in a bull market isn't anything to get excited about, a point that is also lost on most journalists when they write about the plans. After a 1997 *Wall Street Journal* article during a bull market titled "Waking Up Rich: Retirement Accounts Stashed in Stocks Make Employees Millionaires," Ted Benna, the creator of the 401(k) plan, wrote an article in a benefits publication that served as a "correction" to the *Journal* piece. Most likely Benna was forced to do so because the *Journal* refused to publish his letter or op-ed because it would be an exposé of a poorly researched article.

"Frankly, I have been amazed at the attention that the recent *Wall Street Journal* article about 401(k) millionaires has received," Benna wrote in *Compensation and Benefits Review*. "The average account balance for these participants is generally regarded to be around $35,000. Study after study indicates that the average participant is not saving enough for retirement. As a result, the major concern of most knowledgeable individuals is that we may be facing a serious retirement crisis.... In fact, ever since 401(k) plans began, they have been attacked as not being real retirement plans."

Even if the average account balance were $1 million, it doesn't make you a millionaire—it's the minimum for those earning $100,000 at age 65. What's tragic about *The Wall Street Journal* article is that the employees in the article were among the tiny minority in the United States who have accumulated what they need for a secure retirement—for example, a human resource manager pulling down a $100,000 salary who had $1 million in his account. But because the mutual fund companies aren't required to communicate what size nest egg is necessary to be able to retire, he didn't realize that $1 million is the minimum needed to replace 70% of a $100,000 salary for 20 years or more, as opposed to a windfall. So he decided to cash out part of his 401(k) account to buy a sports car.

Another 55-year-old couple with a combined annual income of $200,000 decided that their $800,000 joint account balance was a windfall and quit their jobs, paying $180,000 for a 42-foot boat—when in reality they needed to pass up on yacht purchases and stay in the workforce in order to save up a minimum of $2 million to replace their incomes. As a result of these self-defeating maneuvers, those profiled in the article will end up in the same or worse predicament as those participants who don't have the resources to save enough.

The Wrong 401(k) Reform: Replacing an Employer Match with Taxpayer-Subsidized Investments

One of the problems with the field of finance is that remedies to problems are too often viewed through an ideological lens, rather than a logical one—resulting in a lack of "evidence-based finance." For example, many Democrats typically view stocks as scary and reckless and bonds as safe and secure—witness AARP's lobbying efforts against privatizing Social Security. And many Republicans view the stock market as magical—witness the popularity of Jim Cramer's *Mad Money* TV show.

Unfortunately, like just about everything else in life, the truth is somewhere in the middle. Over the long haul, everyone needs to own stocks because you are a part owner of companies whose shares will be worth many multiples of what they were when you first bought them once you retire. Over the short haul, as you get closer to retirement you need to convert to cash equivalents, such as money market accounts, because stock values run the risk of short-term slumps. On the other hand, nobody should own government bonds because they are a long-term investment whose premiums are generally less than the rate of inflation, so you're actually losing money. The proof is in the pudding: Examining 20-year-holding investment periods from 1926 to 2001, large-company stocks yielded better than 5% returns in all but 19 of the 56 holding periods. In contrast, long-term government bonds lost money in all but eight of the holding periods.

If logic had trumped partisan ideology during the debate over privatizing Social Security when former President George W. Bush tried to overhaul it in 2005, its shortfall would have been addressed by a combination of tax increases and a shift of much of its assets into stock index funds rather than stuck in poorly performing short-term and long-term government bonds, as is currently the case. Rather than privatizing Social Security and allowing investors to shoot themselves in the foot by attempting to time the market with brokerage accounts as Bush proposed (some say at the behest of the brokerage industry), the assets would be managed by a government-sponsored enterprise that would invest in a mix of stock and money market index funds, as is the case with the Thrift Savings Plan, which covers many government employees. Unfortunately, since the Social Security Administration is scheduled to take in fewer taxes than the benefits it pays out starting in 2016, a combination of a lack of a bipartisan dialogue and ignorance about finance has produced another retirement disaster.

So it's no surprise that this lack of financial literacy on the part of Congress and some who purport to be financial experts surfaced during the stock market slump in October 2008. There was a brief media flurry over whether 401(k) plans were working, but the attention was directed not at the paltry employer match but at the misguided notion that stocks they hold are risky and shouldn't be in the plans, despite the fact that they dominate the assets in pension plans.

Testifying before the House Committee on Education and Labor on October 7, 2008, Teresa Ghilarducci, an economics professor, proposed replacing 401(k) employer matching contributions with an annual government deposit of $600 that would be invested both in "safe and risky" investments whose investment returns would be subsidized by the taxpayers, along with requiring that employees contribute 5% of their pay into these investments.

However, replacing an employer contribution with a one-size-fits-all $600 government contribution would devastate nest eggs for 95% of Americans—and the other 5% are probably poor enough that Social Security replaces most of their income at retirement.

Another academic who is frequently quoted in the media on pension matters also appears to use faulty math to address the empty nest egg dilemma. Alicia Munnell, who heads up the Center for Retirement Research, appears to have come to the conclusion that all Americans need to do is work two to four years longer. She says that "in theory workers could accumulate substantial wealth" simply by contributing 6% of pay at age 30 and ending up with a nest egg of $380,000. Why she thinks this one-size-fits-all number would equal retirement adequacy is not clear since it works only if the person's income near retirement is $38,000 ($380,000 equals ten times pay at an income level of $38,000). Since the median income for that age group is around $65,000, these calculations don't add up.

Auto-Enrollment: Better Than No Reform, but Not a Cure for Pension Poverty

The only reform to 401(k) plans has been to automatically enroll employees in an inadequate plan rather than requiring employers to contribute more to these workers' accounts. The Pension Protection Act (PPA) of 2006 makes it easier for plan sponsors to automatically enroll their employees at a starting contribution rate of 3%, which can be raised by at least 1% of salary per year until it reaches 6%. However, although auto-enrollment will give people nest eggs that are better than nothing, it won't fill them.

The problem with the preceding formula is twofold: *First, a 3% starting contribution rate is too low for everybody.* It's less than one-third of the rate required at a starting age of 25 and less than one-seventh for a starting age of 40—and these scenarios assume an employer match! *Second, auto-enrollment keeps the default rate artificially low for job changers, at least for those enrolled in a plan that would have raised their contribution rate each year.* For example, workers who changed jobs every seven years would accumulate only 40% of what they'd need—and that's assuming an employer match at each job. Job changers working for companies without a matching contribution would accumulate less than one-third of what they need.

To make matters worse, employers aren't required to adopt auto-enrollment, and the ones that have adopted it typically don't enroll current employees who aren't participants, only new hires. Nearly two-thirds of employers use automatic enrollment only with new hires, according to a survey of almost 5,500 plans by Plansponsor.com, a retirement research firm in Stamford, Connecticut. In addition, they enroll employees at a "default" contribution rate that is lower than what they would have saved on their own. A Vanguard Group study shows that employees tend to save at an average rate of 2.9% when they are auto-enrolled, versus a 5% rate under voluntary enrollment.

Unfortunately, unless there is a public uproar—instructions for participating in it are included in the next chapter—the best the Obama Administration may do is require auto-enrollment rather than mandating higher employer contributions. The director of the Office of Management and Budget, Peter Orszag, is a proponent of auto-enrollment, having co-authored a book, *Aging Gracefully*, that promotes it. President Obama has also called for requiring employers that don't offer a retirement plan to enroll employees in a "direct deposit" IRA account, covering the 75 million people who don't have plans. Again, President Obama's intentions are good, but as is the case with auto-enrollment, simply enrolling employees in a plan that requires them to foot the bill for their retirement is unheard of in other advanced countries. All companies except those run by the self-employed in Australia are required to contribute an equivalent of 9% of pay into their employees' accounts.

Automatic Annuitization: Ripping Off People Who Can't Afford to Retire

Not only has the mutual fund industry avoided the responsibility for telling their 401(k) clients how much to save in their accounts to achieve their goals, but many of the fund companies and their counterparts in the insurance industry have no compunction about selling annuities or other investment products such as managed payout funds to Baby Boomers who have reached retirement age without sufficient retirement assets. An incorrectly headlined front-page article in *The Wall Street Journal*, "Golden Years: As Boomers Retire, Insurers Aim to Cash In," described the insurance industry's push to sell annuities to retiring Baby Boomers despite a "checkered past" because of high fees, churning, and other issues. According to the *Journal*, sales of variable annuity products have increased more than 50% from 2002 to 2007.

Along with conveying the false impression that most people can afford to retire from a 401(k) plan, the article never addresses the most problematic potential feature of annuities: They can't make empty nest eggs full. The function of an annuity is to make your *adequate* retirement savings last a lifetime even if you live to age 100 or more. If you haven't accumulated enough, you need to keep working—a fact that sellers are not required to disclose to their customers.

Unfortunately, some pension advocates are favoring "automatic annuitization," which means that workers with inadequate nest eggs will be sold a costly product that won't enable them to retire—what's more it's likely that an unscrupulous insurance broker will try to earn commissions by selling annuity owners a new one shortly thereafter.

The so-called Retirement Security for Life Act of 2007, most likely dreamed up by the annuity industry and introduced in 2007 by Representatives Stephanie Tubbs Jones (D-OH) and Phil English

(R-PA) and the ultimately defeated Sen. Gordon Smith (R-OR), would amend the Internal Revenue Code so that 50% of the income generated by the annuity would be excluded from tax; for the typical retiree the tax break would be up to $5,000.

The tax deduction, however, could be totally offset by the fees and frequently deceptive sales practices of the industry; the misdoings by some annuity salespeople include misleading investors about investment returns and how soon investors can access the money, along with generating commissions by convincing the customer to buy a new annuity. What's more, the product isn't even necessary, because the mutual fund industry offers an investment product called a managed payout fund that accomplishes the same goal at a lower cost.

In 2006, the National Association of Securities Dealers (now Financial Industry Regulatory Authority) issued an investor alert regarding annuity salespeople who conducted workplace seminars in which they convinced employees to retire early, cash out of their 401(k) accounts—and very likely causing them to pay "penalty taxes" if they were under age 59½—and open an IRA that consists of a variable annuity. In one disciplinary case that NASD prosecuted, the broker told the employees, "You can make as much in retirement as you can at work," saying that he could generate annual investment returns of 18% and assumed annual returns of 11% to 14%—which no investment can guarantee.

What follows are just a few of the numerous examples of actions taken against annuity sellers in various states.

- In 2008, Florida Governor Charlie Crist signed a law increasing penalties on annuity salespeople who pressure clients to buy annuities they don't need or want. The law increases fines from $100,000 to as much as $150,000 for certain "unfair or deceptive annuity sales activities," including "twisting," in which a salesman lies about the benefits of his annuity to get clients to sell their current annuity from a different company, or "churning," which involves replacing the annuity they have with a new product from the same company.

- In 2006, New York Attorney General Eliot Spitzer announced an agreement in which the Hartford Financial Services Group would pay $20 million in restitution and fines and implement reforms designed to bring fair play and transparency to the marketing of retirement products.

  "This investigation shows how payoffs and deception influenced major deals for retirement products," Spitzer said. The Hartford Financial Services Group also reached an agreement with Connecticut Attorney General Richard Blumenthal.

- In 2005, New Jersey launched its Senior Citizen Investment Protection Act, which limits how long annuity sellers can impose surrender charges in the event the annuity owner wants to sell the product.

How did an industry with such a shameful track record manage to convince some members of Congress to help boost its revenues? Along with the fact that campaign contributions from the insurance industry often influence decisions made by Congress, the industry was probably able to dupe nonprofit organizations representing women and minorities into supporting the legislation, thereby giving it credibility. It probably could do so because the annuitization option does shine a spotlight on one of the more unfortunate features of 401(k) plans, which is that unlike most defined benefit pensions, retirees with 401(k) accounts can and often do take their payments as a lump sum—even before they've reached age 59½, causing them to have to pay taxes and penalties. With no good advice, they might spend the money foolishly rather than banking it and taking payments that will last a lifetime—or, more likely, banking it and continuing to work, which most of us need to do.

Unfortunately, neither the advocacy organizations nor Smith and his co-sponsors appear to have researched the track record of the industry before buying into the idea that an annuity is the solution to this problem. For one thing, for the tiny percentage of 401(k) participants who have saved enough, there are other options for providing income streams for life. For example, the mutual fund industry offers "managed payout" or "target distribution" mutual funds that feature lower fees than their annuity counterparts. What's more, the mutual fund companies offering these products don't employ salespeople who "twist" or "churn" the funds to generate sales commissions.

Bottom line: Anyone who is turning retirement age and is looking at a 401(k) account that's significantly less than ten times their salary needs to keep working—that is, stay in the "accumulation phase" of investing until they have reached that goal, in which case they can study their best options in the "distribution phase." There is no investment product that can turn a "sow's ear" nest egg into a silk purse.

401(k) Security Act: Mandatory 9% Contribution for Companies with Ten or More Employees, Government Contribution for the Rest

Rather than continuing to "reform" defined benefit plans out of existence by putting too many shackles on them, we should work to improve 401(k) plans because they are the right plan for the 21st-century U.S. worker, who switches jobs an average of every four years—the highest turnover rate in the world. Someone with that job-changing history who worked exclusively for companies with only a traditional pension could end up never being vested in any plan—that is, pensionless.

To make a 401(k) plan walk, talk, and quack like a defined benefit plan but without the counterintuitive DB shackles, we should require that companies that are successful enough to have at least 10 employees contribute the equivalent of 9% of pay as Australian employers do, to an account that is portable when the employee leaves work. We should also propose a program that features a *government* contribution for those companies with nine or fewer employees, along the lines of the Universal 401(k) Plan proposed by Michael Calabrese of the New America Foundation (Disclosure: Calabrese was on my company's board of directors when it was a nonprofit). More than 70 million American workers don't participate in a tax-subsidized, payroll deduction saving plan. Calabrese observes that although 65% of full-time workers at firms with more than 100 employees participate in retirement plans, that rate sinks to 45% at firms with fewer than 100 employees and 25% at firms employing fewer than 25.

Calabrese's Universal 401(k) plan would give every employee of a small company an Individual Career Account in which the government would match voluntary contributions by workers and their employers with refundable tax credits deposited directly into their accounts.

As is the case with Australia's version of the 401(k), the country already has an employer-based government-matching program for low-income workers in place called the "co-contribution." On top of the mandatory 9% of pay that workers at *all* employers regardless of size receive to their super accounts, Australians who earn less than $28,980 receive a $1.50 match from the government for every $1 the workers contribute, up to a total of $1,500; co-contributions reduce as income increases, phasing out completely at $58,980.

We Are on a "Countdown to 2011"

In a nutshell, we are looking at a retirement nightmare. The first wave of Baby Boomers, those born in 1946, is scheduled to retire in 2011 and can't afford to—at the same time my daughter's generation, one of the largest in history, is scheduled to graduate from college. Will a big percentage of the 4 million graduates wind up jobless because my generation's 3.4 million Boomers can't afford to retire? We're witnessing a "perfect storm" of pension-poor Boomers, who will need to stay on the job, resulting in potentially jobless Gen Yers, many of whom also have college loans to pay off.

We need a public groundswell to get President Obama to enact the 401(k) Security Act described in this chapter. The next chapter lays out more details of the Act, what you can do to get the Obama Administration to enact it, and some smart 401(k) investing steps you can take in the meantime.

Chapter 2

How to Save Wisely Until We Get 401(k) Reform and How to Make Reform Happen

Those of you who are fortunate enough to work for an employer who offers a regular pension—known as a defined benefit plan—may feel less pressure to save in your 401(k) plan, if your employer offers one. But I wouldn't count on defined benefit plans because, as I pointed out earlier, in the same fashion that the economic meltdown has induced many employers to suspend their matching contributions to 401(k) plans, increasing numbers of companies are "freezing future accruals" to defined benefit plans, which means you'll stop earning benefits and new hires won't get any benefits.

In addition, while some of you may be fortunate enough to work for companies that offer generous profit-sharing plans in addition to 401(k) plans—about 10% of employers offer them—in the same way that matching contributions can be suspended to 401(k) plans, a weak economy can wipe out profits for many companies.

Unfortunately, until meaningful pension reform happens on Capitol Hill, most of us will probably have to work longer, unless you're in your 20s and can afford to save 10% of your take-home pay—especially if you're single and can depend on only one income.

My approach to saving for retirement is Keep It Simple. For the most part, you have to obey some basic rules. Invest mostly in stocks, gradually shifting your allocation to money market funds as you approach retirement age. Avoid brokerage accounts (in which you trade shares of stocks) because you can't time the market. Don't sell in a stock market downturn. Don't cash out, that is, tap into your 401(k) savings, when changing jobs. And that's it. While I've got friends in the financial planning industry, it's an industry that should have been automated and replaced by software, much as software has replaced CPAs to prepare tax returns—witness the wildly popular TurboTax.

At the end of this chapter, I discuss the action plan that's needed to get the solution to the crisis on President Obama's radar screen so that Americans will no longer have to bankroll their own retirement. In the meantime, here are some quick and dirty rules to enable you to put a smart investing strategy on autopilot.

Rule 1: Work Longer, and Both Spouses May Have to Work

If you're part of a married couple, you should expect that both of you will have to work and one spouse will have to save most of his or her paycheck; but at least you'll have the power of two paychecks to feather your nest egg—that is, unless both incomes are needed to meet all living expenses. Needless to say, both of you should contribute the maximum to your 401(k) accounts.

Although the length of time you need to work will vary by individual, assume that if you are a Baby Boomer you will probably need to work another eight to ten years, even if 401(k) reform takes place, because you will have fewer years to benefit from the increased employer contributions and investment returns on them.

Rule 2: Don't Sell in a Downturn

Along with being clueless about whether their clients can retire, most mutual fund companies—with the Vanguard Group being the exception—neglect to tell investors not to "rush to the exits" when the stock market is in turmoil. As former Securities and Exchange Commissioner Arthur Levitt says, "(Brokers) want you to buy stocks you don't own and sell the ones you do...They earn commissions even when you lose money."

In a logical world, the Securities and Exchange Commission (SEC) would require anybody in the investment community to convey a buy-and-hold message—along with revoking the licenses of the brokers who profit by conveying the opposite message. In the same way that lives can be lost in a stampede when someone shouts "fire" in a crowded theater, fortunes can be lost when investors stampede out of the stock market and stay out.

The inconvenient truth about investing is that often when the stock market slumps it's not a setback, it's simply a "bad stock day." Take the stock market swoon of October 19, 1987, the largest one-day slump in history, causing millions of investors to stampede out of the market and stay out. However, a mere two years later the S&P 500 turned in a whopping return of more than 30%—one of only 18 calendar years since 1926 that the market performed that well.

Have investors learned anything in a couple of decades?

Nearly 20 years after the 1987 slump, on hearing bad stock market news in March of 2007, thousands of 401(k) investors moved half a billion dollars out of stock mutual funds into fixed income funds. Unfortunately, two scant months later the S&P 500 closed above 1500 for the first time in more than six years, the longest run of bullishness since 1944.

Why is it self-destructive to head for the exits during a market slump? Because the market isn't falling apart, its shares are temporarily dropping in value. If you react by selling your shares in a downturn and then wait for an upturn to invest again, you'll end up paying top dollar for your shares and buying fewer shares. If, on the other hand, you stay invested, you'll wind up buying more bargain-basement-priced shares that will eventually rise in value, boosting your nest egg.

In fact, some of the biggest stock market booms during the past eight decades have occurred right after the so-called busts. In the 17 calendar years since 1926 that the Standard & Poor's 500 has produced better than 30% returns, eight of these bullish years followed a year of negative returns—most likely because the savvy bargain hunters bought cheap stocks dumped by not-so-savvy investors, causing the share prices to swoon.

What's more, what's rarely mentioned about the Depression is that although there were negative investment returns between 1929 and 1931, the S&P 500 turned in some of the best returns on record during that decade: 53.99% in 1933, 47.67% in 1935, 33.92% in 1936, and 31.12% in 1938. Not only are the 1933 returns the highest on record, there have been only four calendar years in the 83-year stock market history when the S&P 500 has generated better than a 40% return and only 18 calendar years when it has generated better than a 30% return.

The funny thing about the stock market is not only that it's impossible to predict when it's going to be up, but that many of the eye-popping double-digit returns happen during a tiny percentage of the time, which is why you can't time the market. For example, investors who missed the 40 best days in the decade 1994–2004 would have lost 3.23% instead of gaining 12.09% if they had stayed fully invested. Go out even further and the stats are even more mind-boggling: Investors who missed the best 90 days between 1962 and 1993 would have lost 95% of market gains. To put it another way, a dollar would have been worth $24 for the buy-and-hold investor but only $2.10 for the investor who "timed it wrong."

Rule 3: Change Your Investment Strategy as Your "Time Horizon" Changes—That Is, When You Get Closer to Retirement, Not When the Stock Market Changes

Does ignoring market slumps mean that you should never change your 401(k) investment strategy? No—but your decision to change your strategy should be driven by how close you are to retirement and not yesterday's or today's news. Specifically, while younger 401(k) investors in their 20s and 30s should have a higher concentration in stock mutual funds—80% to 100%—that concentration should shrink as investors hit their 40s and 50s, shifting to bond mutual funds or money market funds (my preference is for the latter, as explained in the last chapter). One of the no-brainer ways to accomplish this shift is to move your 401(k) investments into a target date fund if your employer's plan offers one, as I'll detail later, which does the shifting automatically.

Rule 4: Choose a Roth 401(k) If Your Employer Offers One

As of 2006, employers can offer a Roth 401(k) option, in which participants pay taxes on the income contributed today in exchange for tax-free withdrawals at retirement instead of making tax-deductible contributions, which is the case with regular 401(k) accounts. Although some employers have been reluctant to embrace the Roth option—one recent survey found that only around 22% of employers were planning to offer it—my question is: Why do we have anything else *but* Roths from the get-go?

Let's face it, there's a reason for senior citizens discounts—it ain't easy living on a fixed income. With the Roth option, you "get taxes over with" when you can afford to pay them because you are working. Then at retirement you owe Uncle Sam nothing on either your contributed income or your years of investment returns. In contrast, if you have a traditional 401(k) account you've got a huge tax bill when you start withdrawing from your nest egg—not just on contributions but also on investment earnings. Here's an example of the tax hit for a retiree who participates in a traditional 401(k) plan: Let's say a 30-year-old—we'll call him Tom—contributes $5,200 a year to a Roth 401(k), with annualized earnings of 7% a year, accumulating more than $860,000 by age 67—all tax free. However, if Tom had contributed that same amount to a regular 401(k) account over that same period, at a 25% income tax rate Tom would owe more than $230,000 in federal taxes on withdrawals at retirement—and that's potentially on top of state and local income tax. Admittedly, the taxes aren't paid all at once, but it's still a hefty bill when you're living off savings.

Rule 5: Contribute the Maximum, Avoid Auto-Enrollment, and Save Outside of Your Plan

As I mentioned earlier, until my reform gets passed, 401(k) accounts alone aren't going to get Americans on track for retirement. But that still shouldn't stop you from saving as much as you can. If it turns out your employer automatically enrolled you at a 3% contribution rate, contact your service provider and arrange to increase the rate to as much as you can afford, up to the current limits.

If you're part of a two-income household, not only should both of you contribute the maximum allowed to your accounts, but if you can afford to, consider setting aside savings outside of your plan in a Roth IRA and in non-tax-favored investment accounts. Unfortunately, the income and contribution limits on Roth IRAs make it necessary for many people to save in non-tax-favored plans.

Rule 6: Develop a Low-Cost, Buy-and-Hold, Common-Sense Investment Strategy

You basically need to stay invested mostly in stocks until middle age, stick with large-company stocks, and reduce costs and improve investment returns by choosing index funds over managed funds. Here are six simple steps to achieve your goals:

Step 1: For the most part, stick with stocks.

For some strange reason, people who are not "risk tolerant" are advised to stay out of stocks. This is nonsense. For most of your life, most of your money should be invested in stocks. As a part owner of several companies, you're placing a bet that your shares will be worth much more when you're ready to sell them 20, 30, or 40 years from now. On average, you will double your money every seven or eight years if you leave it in stocks. On the other hand, bonds and cash-equivalent investments such as money market funds don't perform as well as stocks because the issuer of the bonds/money market funds "controls the coupon" on their investment returns and inflation can devour these returns. For example, if you're investing in a certificate of deposit or money market fund that pays 2% and the inflation rate is 3%, you're losing money.

Step 2: Diversify by investing in many stocks—that time-honored notion of putting your eggs in different baskets.

The best way to decrease your risk of losing money over the long term is by diversifying, or dividing your money among many stocks; the best way to do this is to invest in mutual funds. The more stocks you own, the more likely that most of the stocks in your portfolio will be winners.

Step 3: Reduce risks by investing in mutual funds that "bet on companies with winning track records": large-company stocks.

If you're lucky enough to own a crystal ball, you can make more money investing in the new-kid-on-the-block companies that are plowing their profits back into their businesses than in the old reliable ones. The successful small companies of today will become the Wal-Marts, Amazons, and Apples of tomorrow. However, there's a downside of investing in a small company: Few of us can predict which companies are going to be the next Google and which are going to be the next failed dot-com. Half of all new companies go out of business within five years of start-up. So instead of betting on a long shot, a safer strategy is to bet on the winners: mutual funds that invest in large-company stock funds, commonly known as large-cap funds.

Step 4: Reduce costs and improve returns by buying "generic"—index funds versus managed funds.

As far as which funds you should invest in, my preference is for index funds, or passive investing, which involves buying and holding a broad array of stocks in their proportion to the overall market rather than buying only those stocks that a fund manager believes are likely to outperform the market.

Index funds are like generic drugs when it comes to large-cap funds. You know how when a prescription drug first hits the market, it can cost an arm and a leg? However, after the patent runs out, other drug companies can copy the formula for it and sell it cheaply—or at least more cheaply than the original version. I would describe the S&P 500, which encompasses the 500 American companies with the greatest market value of stock outstanding, as the "generic equivalent" of a mutual fund made up of large company shares. Why? You're pretty much going to invest in the same companies whose shares are in the managed fund without paying extra for the salaries of the fund managers.

Step 5: If you do choose a target maturity mutual fund, also known as a life-cycle fund, put *all* of your money in this fund.

Target date or target maturity funds are set up to shift your allocation away from stocks and toward fixed-income investments as you get closer to retirement. This is a good idea but many participants are using them the wrong way: A Vanguard study showed that 60% of 401(k) participants who used target date funds invested in more than one target date fund. If you choose a target date fund, all of your money should be in this fund. Needless to say, if your employer offers an S&P 500 target date index fund, that's your best choice.

Step 6: If you can find a target fund that includes international stocks, go for it.

Although the average American is very likely wearing jeans sewn in China, grinding coffee beans grown in Columbia, talking on a cell phone made in Finland, and driving a Japanese car, it's very unlikely that her 401(k) investing money is going where her spending money is. Only one-third of 401(k) participants invest in international funds.

One of the untold stories of globalization in the 21st century is that two-thirds of the world's largest publicly held companies are based overseas—and have been since *Fortune* magazine launched the Global 500 ranking in 1989. It was a different story—at least for the top 50 companies only a few years earlier in 1982—with 23 American firms making the list compared to 17 today.

Although consumers hate paying through the nose to fill their gas tanks, investors might as well reap some payback. 401(k) savers who invest only in the S&P 500 will "own" only six oil companies, missing out on the investment gains of 22 others—a French petroleum refiner is one of the world's biggest companies, rocketing up 43 notches in just a year. And although there's always the risk of business failure wherever you put your money, a lot of the European-based biggies have been around for decades, if not centuries.

Rule 7: Avoid Borrowing from Your 401(k) Account

Although it may be tempting to borrow from your 401(k) account because there's no credit check and there may be a lower interest rate compared to other loans, consider the "cost" of the loan to your retirement future. First, your retirement money should be "working for you," that is, earning investment returns. Second, if you leave your job, your entire loan balance may be due when you can't afford to pay it back—and the tax penalties could cost you a bundle.

Here's an example of the potential hit on a $5,000 loan, assuming investment returns of 8%, a loan interest rate of 7%, a five-year term, and that you're 35 years from retirement. Even if the loan is repaid on time, you've lost $20,716.94 in investment returns.

Rule 8: Don't Tap into Your 401(k) Account Balance When Changing Jobs

Very often when people leave a job, they "cash out" of their vested 401(k) account balances—or spend part or all of it rather than rolling it over to an account at the new employer or to a rollover IRA. But similar consequences face those who cash out of their account as those who borrow from it. And the better choice is to keep your money working hard for you.

Here's why: Cashing out doesn't just mean potentially spending your retirement money. If you're under age 59½ when you cash out,

Uncle Sam takes 20% of your hard-earned money off the top and collects more when you file your return.

Let's assume you are under age 59½, are in the 25% tax bracket, and live in a state with a 5% income tax, and you "cash out" a 401(k) balance of $20,000. Here's what's left over compared to how much money you might end up with if the amount stayed invested:

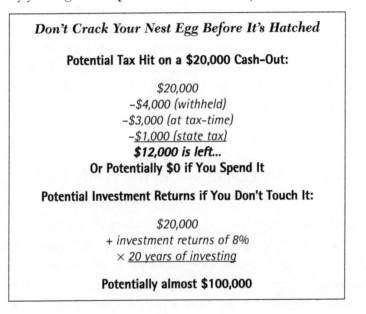

Don't Crack Your Nest Egg Before It's Hatched

Potential Tax Hit on a $20,000 Cash-Out:

$20,000
−$4,000 (withheld)
−$3,000 (at tax-time)
−$1,000 (state tax)
$12,000 is left...
Or Potentially $0 if You Spend It

Potential Investment Returns if You Don't Touch It:

$20,000
+ investment returns of 8%
× 20 years of investing

Potentially almost $100,000

Rule 9: Move Your Old 401(k) Balance to a Rollover IRA, Not Your New Employer's Plan

The best way to keep your retirement money working for you is to roll it over into an IRA at a mutual fund company rather than moving it to the 401(k) plan at your new job or leaving it at your former employer. That's because you keep your retirement money working for you *and* you don't lose track of it.

With Americans changing jobs every four years on average, why deal with the hassle of keeping track of 401(k) accounts at various employers when you can have "one-stop savings" in one IRA. Keeping track of old balances is challenging if one or more of your former employers goes out of business or gets acquired by another company. Even better, unlike a regular IRA, there's no limit to how much money you can save in a rollover IRA as long as the money started out in a qualified retirement plan such as a 401(k). The other reason a rollover IRA is a good idea is that you have more investment choices; for example, your new employer may not offer an index fund as one of its 401(k) investment choices, whereas most mutual fund companies offer them as an IRA investment option.

Rule 10: Get Congress and the White House to Pass the 401(k) Security Act

The bad news is that currently most Americans can't afford to retire from a 401(k) plan. The good news is that there is a new administration in the White House and President Obama seems to understand that most Americans are under severe financial stress. On January 30, 2009, he announced the initiation of a Middle Class Task Force, headed up by Vice President Joe Biden, to address the financial stress facing most Americans, with its five goals including "protecting retirement security." We need to communicate to Vice President Biden that the task before us isn't simply "protecting retirement security" but to boost retirement savings so that people can actually afford to retire.

The reform that we need:

401(k) Security Act: "The 9% Solution"

1. **Coverage mandate.** Every employer with ten or more employees who doesn't offer a regular pension plan—or

whose plan is frozen to new hires—must offer a 401(k) plan and contribute the equivalent of 9% of pay as of 2010. If the 9% contribution rate is challenging in these recessionary times, then we should take a phase-in approach similar to Australia's: start at 5% in 2010, increasing to 7% in 2016 and 9% by 2020.

2. **Employees working in companies with fewer than ten employees would be enrolled in a Universal 401(k) featuring a government contribution.** A new entity, a clearinghouse akin to the Federal Thrift Savings Plan (TSP), which manages very low-cost 401(k)-style accounts for three million federal military and civilian personnel, would receive all deposits.

3. **Get rid of the low ceiling on 401(k) contributions: The limits are $16,500 for those under age 50, $22,000 for those over age 50 in 2009, indexed to inflation.** It makes absolutely no sense to limit how much people can contribute, especially since most of us will have to contribute more to make up for lost time. Baby Boomer Australians can sell a home or another asset and add the proceeds to their accounts; workers over age 60 can make after-tax superannuation contributions of $150,000 a year, or $450,000 over three years.

4. **Disclose the necessary employee contribution "copay."** Participants must be informed what their contribution rate should be depending on their age when they start to save, based on the new requirements. For example, even with the implementation of the new contribution equal to 9% of salary by employers, individuals who start contributing to their accounts at age 25 need to know they should contribute an additional 4%, another 7% if they start at age 30, another 11.25% at age 35, another 17.25% at age 40, and another 42% at age 50.

5. **Employer contributions must start when the employee joins the company, not after one year.** Twenty percent of employers surveyed by Vanguard require eligible employees to have one year of service before the employers match contributions to "minimize compensation costs." This practice could deprive someone who changed jobs every four years of a total of 11 years of investment returns, causing a huge hit to the nest egg.

6. **All employer contributions must be in cash, not company stock.** As was the case with Enron employees, a stock match carries the risk that the contribution will be worthless if the company goes out of business. While the Pension Protection Act has required employers to allow employees with company stock in the plan to gradually diversify out of it, a recent Vanguard study of its clients showed that 8% of employees had more than 80% of their account balances in company stock, revealing a lack of understanding of the risks of not diversifying.

7. **All employers must offer a Roth 401(k) option** and the ability to transfer current balances to a Roth account.

8. **Get rid of discrimination testing:** If highly paid people have waited too long to start saving, they should have the opportunity to save.

9. **Prohibit access to retiree balances until retirement:** At the same time we want employers to contribute more to nest eggs, we want to limit opportunities for employees to "shoot themselves in the foot" by tapping into vested balances before it's time to retire. There should be no loans, hardship withdrawals, or ability to "cash out" when changing jobs. Nearly half of job changers surveyed by Hewitt Associates cashed out of their retirement plans rather than leaving the balances in the old plan or "rolling them over" to an IRA or new plan.

10. **All plans must include an index fund option.**

11. **All plans must include a target fund option, which gradually shifts from stocks to fixed income investments as the participants get closer to retirement.** This should also be the "default" investment if the employee prefers not to choose an investment. Otherwise a participant may make an unwise decision to have a too high allocation in stocks or fixed income investments depending on his or her investment time horizon.

12. **Employers must communicate to workers that they cannot afford to retire unless they have accumulated 10 times their salary in their accounts.**

13. **Workers who have accumulated enough should be encouraged to invest in a managed payout account rather than an annuity.**

Action Plan: First, we need to send a message to Vice President Biden, who heads up the Middle Class Task Force, that the fix that's needed is not simply automatically enrolling Americans in 401(k) plans or IRAs. Americans must deliver the message that only if employers are forced to kick in higher contributions will most folks be able to afford to retire. Along with contacting your own congressperson, go to the contact page on the White House website (http://www.whitehouse. gov/contact/) and submit an email asking Vice President Biden to support the Security Act mandating 9% employer contributions to 401(k) accounts. Here is the URL to the page on my company's website that describes the proposed legislation that can be cut and pasted into your email: http:// www.retirement-solutions.us/401k-nightmare.htm.

Second, contact Rep. George Miller (D-CA), who is chairman of the Health, Education and Labor Committee, which oversees pensions, to seek his support: http://georgemiller.house.gov/contactus/ 2007/08post_1.html.

Third, we also need to send a message to AARP that the advocacy group for retirees needs to do more for would-be retirees who are currently can't-be retirees. When I spoke with a spokesperson for AARP about the retirement crisis, he said that AARP has not been actively involved with retirement security because there hasn't been a hue and cry from the general population. The spokesperson said that to date they have explored "ways in which we can expand access...such as the automatic IRA. We have promoted auto-enrollment. Adequacy is a tougher nut to crack."

Sorry, AARP, as I pointed out in the first chapter, automatically enrolling people in an inadequate savings scheme, whether an automatic IRA or a 401(k), is like giving a cancer patient aspirin instead of chemotherapy. We need to send a "hue and cry" to AARP that if Australians can "crack tough nuts," we need to as well. Contact AARP at http://www.aarp.org/about_aarp/contact/a2003-01-28-contact-issuesform.html and urge them to support my Security Act.

Finally, contact a new organization called Retirement USA that supports retirement reform and is looking for input. While the organization appears to have bought into Ghilarducci's flawed assumption that 401(k) plans are risky, it does favor considering Australia's superannuation system. I urge you contact them at info@retirement-usa.org and ask them to consider my proposed legislation.

The Lobbies That Might Block Reform

As I'll explain in more detail later in the book, one of the reasons why citizen-friendly legislation has a tough time getting passed on Capitol Hill is the huge influence of the business lobby's campaign contributions. Although the bad money fighting retirement reform pales next to that fighting the reform of the mortgage and student lending industries, it's worth knowing who the major players are and how they spend their money.

For the modest 401(k) reforms that have been attempted—fee disclosure, requiring that all employers offer index funds, and abolishing the practice of using company stock as employer matching contributions—it's very likely that the employer lobby has fought against getting rid of stock matches because they are cheaper than cash matches. And the mutual fund industry has lobbied against fee disclosure and the inclusion of index funds because both reforms would justifiably cause most of the industry to lose business, since most managed funds both charge high fees and underperform index funds.

Employer Lobby: According to OpenSecrets.org, **The Coalition on Employee Retirement Benefits (CERB)** was created in 2002 to promote a "cautious approach" to Congressional efforts to reform company retirement plans. The founding members include the National Association of Manufacturers, the U.S. Chamber of Commerce, and the American Benefits Council. It's very likely that their lobbying efforts watered down the Pension Security Act, which merely allows workers to diversify their 401(k) assets by selling company stock within three years of receiving it rather than simply limiting it to no more than 10% of their account assets. In a letter to Sen. Max Baucus (D-MT) and Sen. Charles Grassley (R-IA) of the Senate Finance Committee from CERB's Steering Committee, CERB hints that if Congress is too hard on employers they might stop making the contributions altogether: "[If] employers are not allowed to meet the legitimate business of encouraging employee ownership...they are likely to reduce or eliminate matching contributions."

Expenditures: Finance/Insurance/Real Estate is the largest donor to members of the **House Education and Labor Committee**, which has jurisdiction over 401(k) plans: more than $6.9 million in PAC and individual contributions in the 2008 cycle. The real estate lobby is most likely in favor of the irresponsible practice of allowing "hardship withdrawals" from a 401(k) account for the purpose of buying a first home. The **House Ways and Means Committee**, which opposed Rep. George Miller's bill that would require fee disclosure and the inclusion of index funds, receives most of its contributions from Finance/Insurance/Real Estate: nearly $14 million in the 2008 cycle alone.

PART II

How the American Dream Turned into a Nightmare

The Mortgage Mess: It Ain't Just Subprime—It's Half of Americans in Overpriced Homes

Next to America's pension poverty, the most baffling—and the least talked about—financial mystery is how Americans have managed to live in areas where homes are unaffordable—approximately half of the U.S. population. The recommended prudent ratio of household income to home price is not more than three times income. At the housing bubble's peak in 2007, here's what the ratio was in the following metropolitan areas: a multiple of 11 times the median wage in Boston, 13 in New York, 16 in Los Angeles, and 22 in San Francisco. Even if you assume that these households are two-earner families, the ratio is still too high. Some examples:

- It wasn't long after a young couple bought their modest, 2,000-square-foot house for $730,000 about 25 miles from San Francisco in July of 2004 when panic began to set in. When the couple sat down to do their household budget, it was clear that mortgage and tax payments would consume 55% of their income. The wife told a *Business Week* reporter that at that point, "we almost called the real estate agent and said we wanted to get out."

- In 2007, only 2% of families in Los Angeles were able to afford the median sales price of homes in the region. Even in the most affordable area in the state of California, Chico, only 26.8% of families could afford the median $245,000 home.

- A pair of newlyweds featured in a 2007 *Money* article told the reporter they couldn't really afford their home. The monthly carrying costs on their two-bedroom condo in Arlington, Virginia, ran about $2,500 a month—a whopping $30,000 a year—and they feared their monthly payment could go higher still as their adjustable-rate mortgage reset to a higher rate. They had already taken in a roommate to help pay the bills—not exactly a fun way to start out a marriage. The irony is that the couple should be able to afford the condo, which the wife bought when she was single for $219,000.

What's rarely, if ever, addressed by the media or policy makers are the circumstances that led to so many American homeowners becoming "over their heads in debt." How can a modest 2,000-square-foot home cost nearly $1 million? Why are there yearly carrying costs of $30,000 on a $219,000 home? Where do people live when only 2% of the population can afford a home—is everybody stuck in an apartment or enduring long commutes from an affordable region to work in an expensive region? What's even odder, it's clear that neither of the couples mentioned seems to fit into the "subprime" category, which in general applies to folks with poor credit history—nor were my husband and I when we bought our first home in 1987. How did a couple get approved for a mortgage that consumes 55% of their income?

What's even more amazing is that in the rare instances that housing bubbles were covered by the media before 2008, the debate was whether they existed—which is pretty ridiculous, given the affordability ratios in major metropolitan areas listed previously—not the financial stress that's caused by the people carrying these bubbly mortgages, at a time when most people need all the spare money they can get to save in their 401(k) accounts. Another topic not discussed is the worst-case scenario of the bubble, which is that those who do own unaffordable homes won't be able to find buyers for them once they are ready to retire, destroying much of their nest egg.

We now have another perfect storm as millions of Americans who are stuck with adjustable-rate mortgages they can't afford, but since their home values have dropped they won't be able to refinance to a low fixed rate. Not since the Depression has a larger share of Americans owed more on their homes than they are worth. Nearly 8.8 million homeowners, or 10.3% of the total, were underwater in 2008, more than double the percentage in the preceding year. Although the housing slumps of the mid-1970s and late 1980s were confined to the coasts, the 2008 bust cut a far wider path and came at a time when home debt was at its highest level since World War II.

ARMs: Bait and Switch by Another Name

There are many players in the mortgage shell game: lenders who approved of mortgages on homes the borrowers couldn't afford, brokers who baited and switched borrowers by getting them into unaffordable loans, then collected "prepayment penalties" when the borrowers were forced to refinance, and appraisers who were pressured to inflate home values in order to get paid for an appraisal. Then when the mortgages were securitized, we saw rating agencies give Triple A ratings to investments that should have been rated "Triple F."

The finger of blame was rarely, if ever, pointed at the increasing use of adjustable-rate mortgages (ARMs) by the lending industry; mortgages that are simply bait-and-switch by another name. The loan essentially gets homeowners into homes they can't afford and shifts interest-rate risk to the borrower, misleading them that they can always refinance when interest rates go up, "because home values always go up." To put it another way, an ARM is a "liar's loan," except the originator is doing the lying, not the prospective buyer fabricating his or her income.

It's entirely possible that the mortgage payment on a typical ARM can double within the first three years of the loan, despite the fact that outside of hedge fund managers, actors, and athletes, there are few Americans whose income doubles in such a short period. If homeowners can't refinance because the home value is lower as a result of a bursting bubble, many homeowners lose their homes and neither the banks nor the mortgage brokers are held responsible.

ARMs Cause Homes to Be Unaffordable, Threatening Retirement Security

The worst-case scenario of the potential damage caused by ARMs may be yet to come. By causing home prices to skyrocket to the stratosphere of unaffordability, ARMs may result in homeowners being unable to sell their homes when they are ready for retirement—destroying the "fourth leg" of the four-legged chair that actually makes up most people's retirement, along with Social Security, a pension or 401(k) account, and other savings. Home equity is the most important asset of many elderly households, and for some it's the only significant asset.

So how did this country get into this predicament? Some blame the origins of the bubble on the Depository Institutions Deregulation and Money Control Act of 1980, which allowed lenders to charge higher rates and fees to borrowers, or the Alternative Mortgage Transaction Parity Act of 1982, which allowed the use of variable-interest-rate ARMs and balloon payments.

Until the 1980s, most homeowners got fixed-rate mortgages from banks and thrifts, who financed these loans with low-cost federally insured deposits, and lenders were watched over by regulators. But after the Savings and Loan (S&L) crisis in the 1980s and early 1990s, regulators insisted banks and thrifts hold more capital against risky loans. This tipped the playing field in favor of unregulated lenders, who financed themselves not by deposits but by Wall Street credit lines and by "securitization" of their loans—in effect, the sale of loans to investors. Securitization weakened the link between the lender and the borrower.

Housing Bubble Actually Started in the 1970s with the Death of Low-Income Housing

However, it appears that the housing bubble actually started in the 1970s before the S & L crisis: The largest historic jump in home prices nationwide occurred from 1974 to 1981, when the median price ballooned more than 70%, compared to 45.6% from 2000 to 2005. This spike occurred despite the fact that interest rates on mortgages were at all-time highs; the highest rate on adjustable-rate mortgages since Freddie Mac has been keeping records, 16.63%, occurred in 1981.

Why? Skyrocketing inflation, which first reared its ugly head in 1973, meant banks had to charge higher interest rates because it cost them more to borrow money from the Fed. At the same time, banks lobbied state legislatures to remove interest-rate ceilings to set them more in line with money market realities.

Unfortunately, when you're a president and the going gets tough in the economy, you look for ways to trim the federal budget. The target: low-income housing. Richard Nixon may be remembered for the Watergate scandal, but his most damaging legacy wasn't eavesdropping on his political enemies or breaking into the Democratic Party headquarters but slashing government subsidies for low-income housing. Subsidies that produced more than 300,000 units annually for low- and middle-income families vanished altogether in January 1973 under a Nixon Administration moratorium, so home ownership was the only choice for low-income families who previously would have qualified for subsidized housing.

Also, the introduction of rent control made low-income housing unprofitable for home builders, since rents did not keep pace with construction costs. Rental apartment units, which accounted for about one million starts in 1972, dropped to an annual rate of 236,000 in 1975. As a result, 85% of the population couldn't afford a typical home in 1975. In 1977, Housing Secretary Patricia Harris announced the appointment of a task force to deal with the fact that the median price for a new home had risen a whopping 89% in seven years, calling it a "crisis."

A 1980 *New York Times* article titled "America's New Levittowns" described the rise of the condominium industry as a direct result of home unaffordability: "The cost of a conventional single-family home on its own lot has risen so fast in recent years that many Americans who do not already own one never may."

Then Ronald Reagan continued Nixon's policies of cutting low-income housing expenditures. While Jimmy Carter had budgeted $32 billion for low-income housing in 1979, in 1988 Reagan slashed the budget to less than $8 billion. As a result, construction of new public housing fell by 90% by 1989.

Although cutting the supply of any commodity usually causes its price to rise when there's' strong demand, if most people can't afford housing you would think that prices would go down—how did people qualify for homes that they couldn't afford? The bubble also occurred during a period of high unemployment rates: The 7.6% unemployment rate in 1981 is the fifth highest in the 59 years that the Bureau of Labor Statistics has been keeping records. It also occurred during a period of wage stagnation: Although income adjusted for inflation rose 38% in the 1950s and 33% in the 1960s, it dropped 9.2% between 1973 and 1982 alone.

Despite the fact that the vast majority of Americans can't afford to buy a home, while the median home price was a little more than three times the median wage in 1976, a mere five years later it was more than four times the median wage, and it's currently six times the median wage.

Do the Chairmen of the Fed Know Anything About Economics?

Incredibly, despite the fact that a housing bubble has been in existence in the U.S. for more than 30 years, the economists who are in charge of running our economy have appeared clueless that the dilemma exists. While Former Federal Reserve Chairman Alan Greenspan's role in wrecking the economy has now tarnished his legacy—in October of 2008 Greenspan was excoriated by the House Oversight and Government Reform Committee for his 20-year track record of opposing regulation and enabling the housing and internet bubbles—current Fed chairman Ben Bernanke's denial of it should sully his.

At Bernanke's confirmation hearings as Fed chairman in November of 2005, Sen. Paul Sarbanes (D-MD) pointed out that the number of people taking out adjustable-rate mortgages soared in 2004. "Are you concerned about the potential for a bubble in the housing market?" the senator asked Bernanke. His reply: The Fed was reviewing its guidelines for these loans and planned to issue new ones soon.

Three months earlier, as chairman of the Council of Economic Advisers, Bernanke told the media he wasn't concerned about the bubble because of the strong economy: "House prices are being supported in very large part by strong fundamentals....We have lots of jobs, employment, high incomes, very low mortgage rates, growing populations, and shortages of land and housing in many areas."

His remarks are nothing short of astounding, given that wages have grown more slowly than inflation in the past 20 years and that shortages of land and housing cause home prices to rise rather than allowing them to be affordable. He also appears to have been unaware that actual interest rates paid by borrowers with a typical ARM cause the monthly payments to be so unaffordable that homeowners lose their homes. Finally, Bernanke seems unaware that a big portion of the "lots of jobs" created in the first part of the 21st century were "fake" jobs created by the housing bubble; nearly one million jobs were real estate related.

In the almost two years that followed—until late August of 2007, in fact—the Fed sang a similarly confident tune, just as it had for most of Greenspan's last years as chairman. In 2006, Bernanke predicted that housing would "most likely experience a gradual cooling rather than a sharp slowdown."

Interest-Only Mortgages Are the Worst Kind of Bait and Switch

One of the reasons the bubble is bursting now is the increasing use of interest-only loans, which essentially allow borrowers to repay only the interest in the beginning years of the loan, delaying for years repayment of any loan principal. The loans are a gamble that home prices will continue to rise at a brisk pace, allowing the borrower to either sell the home at a profit or refinance before the principal payments come due. We've already seen from the 2008–2009 meltdown that the loan is a gamble in which "the house usually wins."

Interest-only loans exploded in popularity in regions where home prices were soaring, including California, Arizona, and Florida. As of 2006, these mortgages accounted for 23% of loans, according to LoanPerformance.com, which tracks data from more than 80% of lending institutions.

The loans are attractive because their initial monthly payments are tantalizingly low—about $1,367 a month for a $320,000 mortgage, compared with about $1,842 a month for a traditional 30-year, fixed-rate loan. However, if home prices fall, borrowers lose big. "It's a game of musical chairs," said Allen J. Fishbein, former director of housing and credit policy at the Consumer Federation of America. "Somebody is going to have the chair pulled out from under them when they find prices have leveled out and they try to sell, only to find they can't sell it for what they paid for it."

Mortgage Brokers: Putting the Customer Last

So how did so many homeowners end up with homes that have caused them to be "over their heads" in debt? More puzzling still, why did lenders let them? Part of the cause is the deregulation of the banking industry; underwriting, in which the credit history of the applicant was vetted to ensure that the loan would be repaid, was either replaced by brokers, who are loosely regulated, or standards were lowered.

At the height of the boom, nearly 70% of mortgages were arranged by brokers. The problem is that there are no laws requiring brokers to act in the best interest of borrowers. "We do not solely represent the consumer," says George Hanzimanolis, president-elect of the National Association of Mortgage Brokers.

Some Appraisers Overstate Home Values

In addition, in the same fashion that rating agencies gave risky investments an "AAA" rating, some appraisers were pressured to boost home value estimates in order to compete for business. A 2003 study by October Research Corp. found that 55% of 500 appraisers surveyed nationwide felt pressure to overstate values: half the time they were asked to raise values by 10%, and 41% of the time the request was for between 11% and 20%.

Abolish Adjustable-Rate Mortgages

Until Congress understands the flaws in adjustable-rate mortgages, it will be fooled into thinking that the problem has solved itself—especially if an upturn in home prices masks the inevitable recurrence of the collapse when they slump again.

Perhaps the most baffling and frustrating feature of the mortgage mess is that, to my knowledge, the House Financial Services Committee never held public hearings in which bait-and-switched homeowners testified as to how their mortgage payments doubled in just a few years, or spotlighted the role that brokers played in reassuring them that "they could always refinance because home values always go up." (Or if hearings were held, the media rarely covered them.) As a result, the public outcry was against the minority of borrowers who took out "liar's loans" so that they could flip properties—common in Arizona and Nevada—instead of the bankers, brokers, and rating agencies who enabled this mess.

While AIG's and GM's leaders got called on the carpet for obscene paychecks and their use of corporate jets, to my knowledge, the bankers were not interrogated as to their unconscionable practices. A bait-and-switch mortgage may not meet the same legal definition of a Ponzi scheme as that pulled off by Bernie Madoff, but most of the victims of this practice are similarly devoid of any recourse or rescue, as you'll learn in the next chapter.

In retail sales, a bait and switch is a form of fraud in which the merchant lures customers by advertising a product or service at an unprofitably low price, and then reveals that the advertised good is not available but a substitute is. Courts have held that bait-and-switcher retailers may be subject to a lawsuit.

What's tragic is not only that this law doesn't apply to banks, but that by the time "the switch occurs" the mortgagee can't "walk out of the showroom," as a prospective car buyer can. By the time the borrower realizes she's stuck with "a mortgage lemon," she's facing potential foreclosure or unaffordable prepayment penalties even if she finds a new lender with an affordable low fixed-rate mortgage. It's time to make the lenders, not the borrowers, face the consequences of irresponsible lending practices. In the next chapter we'll look at what kind of reform we need to ensure that bankers put the interests of the borrowers ahead of their own.

Chapter 4

How Laws Protect Banks, Not Borrowers, and the Reform We Need

How did America's mortgage industry become so lawless—the Wild West of finance? Along with Alan Greenspan, on a federal level the finger of blame is probably pointed at former Sen. Phil Gramm (R-TX), who essentially undid the law that Franklin D. Roosevelt enacted that not only succeeded in ending the Depression, but probably played a strong role in preventing future Depressions. Former President Bill Clinton also played a significant role by buying into "lawless enterprise" and signing Gramm's deregulatory legislation into law. On a state and local level, while honest and gutsy politicians attempted to rein in reckless lending, they ended up being defeated by the federal banking regulators who put the banks' priorities over those of the borrowers.

Banks not only lobby against legislation that would force them to lend responsibly, but pay fees to a federal regulator who puts the interest of the banks over that of the borrowers. This is like paying a cop to look the other way when you exceed the speed limit. Even worse, the judges in these cases often side with the banks instead of the borrowers, as I'll detail later in the chapter.

While many federal regulators at least pay lip service to putting consumers first—the Securities and Exchange Commission (SEC), for example, refers to itself as "the investors' advocate"—time and again, the U.S. agency that borrowers might assume is on their side, the Office of the Comptroller of the Currency (OCC), has lined up with banks to fight state and local measures that aid consumers. Banks can choose either a state or a federal regulator; the OCC and state banking departments subsist entirely on fees paid by the institutions they regulate.

Unfortunately, courts have tended to side against the borrowers. That's because judges must follow rules even if they don't make any sense—in this case, it's the National Bank Act of 1863 that authorizes the OCC to oppose any state or municipal attempt to interfere with national banks. In addition, when the OCC goes to court, it invokes a provision in the Constitution known as preemption, a legal doctrine that asserts that federal laws prevail over state laws, even if the result is bad laws or no laws.

The attorneys general of North Carolina and Iowa found that out the hard way in April of 2003 when they traveled to Washington, D.C., to urge Comptroller John D. Hawke, Jr., to give states more latitude to limit exorbitant interest rates and fees that most borrowers don't know about because they're in fine print. Hawke wouldn't budge, insisting he would reinforce federal policies that hindered states from reining in lenders. By doing so, the "OCC took 50 'sheriffs off the jobs' during the time the mortgage lending industry was becoming the Wild West," said Roy Cooper, the attorney general for North Carolina.

"There is no question that preemption was a significant contributor to the subprime meltdown," said Kathleen E. Keest, a former assistant attorney general in Iowa who now works at the Center for Responsible Lending. "It pushed aside state laws and state law enforcement that would have sent the message that there were still standards in place."

Efforts in Georgia to rein in unwise lending provoked a particularly fierce federal reaction. When Roy Barnes was elected governor in 1998, he decided to push through the toughest anti-predatory lending law in the country. The 2002 bill would have made *everybody* in the lending game liable for irresponsible loans, from the mortgage lenders and brokers to the investment banks and rating agencies, if the loans they sold, securitized, or rated were deemed unfair—in other words, creating "assignee liability." Currently these loans are bundled into securities and the lender passes along the risk of default to institutional investors.

Hawke assisted the banking industry in fighting this legislation by issuing a rule in 2003 that the Georgia law did not apply to national banks or their subsidiaries. Then in 2004, Hawke went so far as to say that state-chartered banks were exempt as well.

Unfortunately, Barnes lost his job in the subsequent election, and the lobbyists were swarming over everybody else. The debate during a hearing on the bill turned so nasty that when legal aid attorney William Brennan, a supporter of the legislation, tried to talk legislators into blocking amendments softening the law, Brennan needed a police escort to the hearing because he feared that angry mortgage brokers would block his way.

Not surprisingly, the final legislation sharply curtailed a provision that would create assignee liability. The consequences: Georgia at one point had one of the highest rates of foreclosure in the country.

In 2002, Frank Jackson, then a member of the Cleveland City Council, tried to negotiate with mortgage lenders for more favorable terms after he saw that many lower-income residents were being persuaded to pile on high-interest debt, most likely because they had a lower credit score and were considered risky borrowers. To his surprise, the lenders bypassed him and persuaded the state legislature to enact a less stringent version of an anti-predatory lending act he was drafting. "It was pure greed based on exploitation," he said.

When Jackson tried to get a law passed that affected only Cleveland, a bank trade group sued to block Ohio municipalities from passing lending laws, and the Ohio Supreme Court later sided with the industry. The consequences: More than 80,000 homes were in foreclosure in Cleveland as of 2008, then the highest per capita rate in the country.

The Finger of Blame for Bank Deregulation Is Pointed at Phil Gramm

Along with a lack of strong federal regulation creating assignee liability for investment and mortgage banks, brokers, and rating agencies, the finger of blame for defeating reform and getting rid of good laws can be pointed at former Sen. Phil Gramm of Texas, who sat on the Senate Banking, Housing and Urban Affairs Committee until he retired at the end of the 2002 session. Despite being from an oil state, the vast majority of his campaign contributions came from securities and investment firms and commercial banks, raising more than half a million dollars from them in the five years before he left Congress. From 1989 to 2002, federal records show he was the top recipient of campaign contributions from commercial banks and among the top five recipients of donations from Wall Street.

In late 1999, Gramm played a central role in the Gramm-Leach-Bliley Act, which removed barriers between commercial and investment banks and split up oversight of conglomerates among government agencies. While the SEC would oversee the brokerage arm of a company, bank regulators would supervise the banking operation, and state insurance commissioners would examine the insurance business, no single agency would have authority over the entire company. By doing so, he essentially repealed the Glass-Steagall Act, which established the Federal Deposit Insurance Corporation (FDIC)—along with helping end the Great Depression.

While from 1999 to 2001 Congress considered steps to curb predatory loans—those that typically had high fees, prepayment penalties, and ballooning monthly payments—in 2000 Gramm refused to have his banking committee consider the proposals, an intervention hailed by the National Association of Mortgage Brokers as a "huge, huge step for us." A year later, he objected again when Democrats tried to stop lenders from being able to pursue claims in bankruptcy court against borrowers who had defaulted on predatory loans.

Remember the outrage at the obscene CEO bonuses paid to reckless AIG executives in March of 2009? While Gramm may not have been to blame for the bonuses—that blame appears to fall on his former Democratic colleague, Chris Dodd (D-CT)—he is largely responsible for deregulating the "exotic" financial instruments that led to AIG's downfall.

Nearly all its losses centered on AIG FP, which was essentially a hedge fund that built a portfolio of $2.8 trillion in derivatives that made irresponsible bets on the U.S. real estate market. As Ben Bernanke put it, "AIG exploited a huge gap in the regulatory system...This was a hedge fund, basically, that was attached to a large and stable insurance company."

What's more, with its high credit rating—uh-oh—AIG wasn't required to stockpile reserves or collateral as traditional insurers must to cover potential losses.

Another major player in the deregulatory effort is former SEC Chairman Christopher Cox, who led the effort to rewrite securities laws to make investor lawsuits harder to file, reversed or reduced settlements that companies had agreed to, and dismantled a risk management office that was assigned to watch for future problems.

How the Revolving Door Ensures That the SEC Is Toothless

The other reason mortgage reform doesn't happen is the second-most-corrupting influence in Congress besides campaign contributions: the revolving door. In the same fashion that the OCC puts the interest of banks over that of borrowers, the fact that many congresspeople or folks who work for the SEC wind up working for the very industries they oversee means that they may look the other way rather than enforcing rules. For example, the SEC's most recent director of its enforcement division is the former general counsel of JPMorgan Chase and the enforcement chief before him became general counsel of Deutsche Bank's corporate and investment banking division.

Probably most scandalous of all is that the very man who presided over the bank bailouts—former Treasury Secretary Henry Paulson—lobbied the SEC to get rid of rules that might have prevented the mortgage mess from happening in the first place when he headed up Goldman Sachs. On April 28, 2004, Paulson and the heads of four other investment banks met with the five members of the SEC to convince it to exempt their brokerage units from a regulation that limited the amount of debt they could take on.

Banks Got Help but Most Borrowers Didn't

When Congress delivered a multibillion-dollar bailout to irresponsible banks, it didn't make any requirements as to how the bailout money had to be spent—with the most logical mission being to re-service loans or make new ones.

While Henry Paulson told banks they should "deploy, not hoard" the money, since he didn't make deploying it a condition of the bailout, the banks simply did what they pleased.

At the Palm Beach Ritz-Carlton in November of 2008, the chairman of Whitney National Bank in New Orleans told Wall Street analysts how his bank intended to use its $300 million in federal bailout money. Or, more likely, how it was *not* going to use it. "We're not going to change our business model or our credit policies to...make more loans," he said.

As a result of the lack of strictures, few borrowers were being helped as of early 2009 despite the fact that interest rates on fixed-rate loans fell below 5%, the lowest level since the 1950s. The reason why nearly 70% of borrowers who wanted to refinance wouldn't get approved? Either the borrowers' credit ratings weren't good, they owed more than the value of the house, or they had jumbo mortgages—those above the $625,000 limit that Freddie Mac and Fannie Mae buy or guarantee in high-cost areas as of 2009.

On March 4, 2009, President Obama announced "the most ambitious effort since the 1930s" to help troubled homeowners, offering lenders incentives and subsidies to stop foreclosures. For example, the initiative gave mortgage servicing companies upfront incentive payments of $1,000 for every loan they modified and additional payments of $1,000 a year if the borrower remained current.

But why would any bank leap at these measly $1,000 incentives when they can profit off of the interest rates they are charging current borrowers? Also, while some have suggested that Congress should grant qualifying homeowners the ability to get new government loans based on the current appraised values, my question is why is the government on the hook in the first place? The banks loaned irresponsibly; what should have happened is that the banks should have been **required** to "eat" their losses and revise the terms of the loan so that the homeowners were making mortgage payments that were not higher than 30% of their income rather than being "incentivised" to modify the mortgages.

Canada's Bank Regulator Actually Regulates Banks, Instead of Being Paid to Fight Good Laws

In the same fashion that Australians are actually going to be able to retire from their version of a 401(k) account, Canadians are protected from bait-and-switch mortgage practices.

Because Canada's banking industry is regulated, it hasn't faced a single bank failure, calls for bailouts, or government intervention in the financial or mortgage sectors. In 2008, the World Economic Forum ranked Canada's banking system the healthiest in the world compared to the U.S. ranking of 40th and Britain's ranking of 44th. The reason: Canadian banks lend responsibly and aren't over-leveraged. Canadian banks are typically leveraged at a ratio of 18 to 1 compared to 26 to 1 for American banks.

Not surprisingly, Canada's prudent lending standards result in making homes more affordable. The most expensive city in the country, Toronto, featured an average home price of $374,449 in January of 2008, compared to the median sales price of $459,400 in Los Angeles in the first quarter of 2008, $519,200 in the Greater New York City area, $701,700 in San Francisco, and $780,000 in San Jose.

Canadian citizens benefit from not only a more highly regulated industry but one that educates its citizens about the corrosive influence of mortgage debt rather than profiting from it. The Financial Consumer Agency of Canada's website features a quiz called "Test Your Mortgage Knowledge" that demonstrates to users the effect of "compound interest in reverse" and why it's better to have a shorter loan or "amortization period": (http://www.fcac-acfc.gc.ca/eng/consumers/ITools/Quizzes/MortgageQuiz-eng.asp?sn=0). The results are astounding: Nearly 85% of Canadians surveyed make weekly or biweekly payments to speed up the loan payoff, a third make a lump-sum payment against principal, and nearly four out of five say they want to pay off their mortgages as fast as possible, according to Canada Mortgage and Housing Corp.

Unfortunately, when I did a literature search, I could find no statistics reflecting the percentage of Americans who make biweekly payments or have 15-year mortgages, reflecting on our lack of education about this vital cost-cutting alternative to a conventional mortgage.

Attempts at Reform

In mid-June of 2009 President Obama outlined some proposed reforms that were ambitious enough to annoy the financial services industry but still didn't go far enough. Among other proposals, he wanted to create a new agency to regulate mortgages—or possibly give the Fed oversight responsibilities—along with enabling the government to take over failing banks and requiring that banks hold more capital. While the latter requirement makes sense, giving the Fed more power would be a disaster, given its historic lack of oversight, foresight, or insight into our financial woes, regardless of its chairmen—probably the reason why it was one of the few proposals favored by the banking industry. And the last thing the taxpayers need is to be on the hook for reckless banking decisions.

The good news is that there is a little-known gutsy group of reform-minded Senators who are trying to convince President Obama to go even further and "rewind the tape" by dismantling the deregulatory efforts instigated by Phil Gramm and sanctioned by former President Clinton that got us into this mess. They are Carl Levin of Michigan, Byron Dorgan of North Dakota, Dianne Feinstein of California, Jim Webb of Virginia, Bernie Sanders of Vermont, and Maria Cantwell of Washington, who spearheaded the group.

This "small group of insurgents," as *Newsweek* called them, were among the few who were brave enough to challenge some of Clinton's deregulatory efforts—an effort that takes moxie because, unfortunately, on Capitol Hill it's not "politically correct" to challenge a President's decisions if he's a member of your political party—even if these decisions are harming your constituents.

Sen. Cantwell's zeal for reform is a result of the Enron debacle in 2001, when energy speculators wielding derivatives gouged her constituents out of $1 billion. Then in September of 2008, after Fannie Mae and Freddie Mac nearly failed, Cantwell decided she was "mad and wouldn't take it anymore." In late March of 2009 she and her five "fellow insurgents" met with President Obama and voiced their concerns that too many of his advisers, namely Obama's chief economic adviser Larry Summers and Treasury Secretary Tim Geithner, had bought into the notion that regulation hampers capitalism.

As *Newsweek* writer Michael Hirsh described Cantwell's effort, "(I)t is part of a larger battle for the future of the financial system—and in some ways capitalism itself." Or more precisely, it's a battle to wake up Capitol Hill to the fact that the oxymoron known as the financial services industry has never obeyed the rules of capitalism, unlike its counterparts in virtually every other area of commerce, but prefers to profit by gouging its customers rather than delivering value. We need to haul Wall Street on the carpet and force it to shape up or ship out—not kowtow to it.

Unfortunately, reform of the financial industry is unlikely to happen on Capitol Hill unless we have genuine campaign finance reform—as I'll detail later in the book—AND lock the revolving door between oversight of the financial services industry and a future job in the industry. For example, Sen. Cantwell described Commodity Futures Trading Commission (CFTC) Chairman Gary Gensler as "whining" about how hard it is to get new regulation past Wall Street. As Hirsh put it, "Who is he more worried about: Wall Street or fellow

Democrats like Maria Cantwell?" The answer: most likely the former, since any reform undertaken by Gensler, a former Goldman Sachs executive, will ensure that his resume is tossed in the trash if he wants a job back on The Street after his term is over.

In the next chapter, we'll look at how to manage your mortgage finances, whether you're a current homeowner or a would-be one. In the meantime, here's the reform we need in order to protect homeowners so that the mortgage mess will never happen again.

Reform That's Needed: Abolish Adjustable-Rate Mortgages, Lock the Revolving Door

Action Plan: We need rules that will protect borrowers, not banks. While Barney Frank is in charge of the House Financial Services Committee and voters should urge him to enact reform, I'd highly recommend also contacting one or more of the six senators listed above via their websites and encourage them to support my reform measures—especially if you live in the state that they represent.

Unfortunately, when you go to Frank's Web page, he says that he won't respond to e-mails coming outside of his Massachusetts district—amazing, isn't it, given that his policies affect every American? So I'd recommend snail-mailing him (unfortunately, it will take a month to reach his office because of security issues) and then calling him if snail mail isn't effective: Congressman Barney Frank, 2252 Rayburn Building, Washington, D.C. 20515, (202) 225-5931.

Here's what we need to tell the reform-minded Senators and Barney Frank:

1. Repeal the Alternative Mortgage Transaction Parity Act of 1982, which allows largely unregulated companies to structure their loans as "alternative mortgage transactions" and preempt state protections.

2. Freeze the current rates on adjustable-rate loans and ban ARMs going forward, including interest-only mortgages, which are essentially ARMs by another name.

3. Create assignee liability so that everyone involved in the mortgage business—brokers, rating agencies, banks, and appraisers—are liable.

4. Protect homeowners from becoming house-poor by prohibiting mortgages that exceed three times the borrower's household income.

5. Require mortgage brokers and lenders to disclose the crucial role homeownership plays in retirement equity, thus discouraging unnecessary home-equity loans, cash-out refinancings, and "trading up."

6. Prohibit the OCC from taking fees from banks and require it to exist purely on taxpayer subsidies, as other agencies do.

7. Shut the revolving door between the SEC, the CFTC, and other regulatory agencies and the financial services industry. We taxpayers benefit more from a bureaucrat-for-life than from one whose decisions are compromised by a future job on Wall Street.

What's Blocking Reform

Members of Congress are compromised, either because as members of a committee that drafts legislation they receive campaign contributions from the mortgage and real estate industry, or because they are given "deals" on mortgages by lenders and/or are permitted to vote on legislation that affects the industry even when they have a "second job" in the industry. Specifically:

- Finance/Insurance/Real Estate is the most generous contributor to Congress, donating more than $463.4 million in the 2008 election cycle alone and a whopping $2.2 billion since 1989, according to the Center for Responsive Politics.

- Members of the National Association of Realtors are the third-most-generous givers to politicians: more than $34 million since 1989, according to CRP.

- A 2003 Bush administration proposal for reform to the home mortgage system, strongly supported by consumer groups because it would help them shop for lower fees, was opposed by Sen. Richard C. Shelby (R-AL), who at the time was chairman of the Senate, Banking, Housing and Urban Affairs Committee. Shelby collected nearly $1 million from the real estate industry and $863,000 from commercial banks in the 2007–2008 election cycle. He ranks fourth in the Senate in total contributions from mortgage bankers and brokers. Shelby has raised a total of $20.4 million since the start of his political career; with a net worth between $5.2 million and $35.7 million, he is the 17th-wealthiest member of the Senate.

Chapter 5

The Fix: Refinance to a Fixed-Rate Mortgage; Move to an Affordable Region

In this chapter I'll offer tips for current homeowners and would-be homeowners, including those who can't afford a house in the high-priced region where they currently live.

Tips for Current Homeowners

For those of you who already own a home, if you're currently stuck with an adjustable-rate mortgage (ARM), refinance to a fixed-rate loan if you haven't already, avoid home equity loans (more on that in Chapter 10), and don't waste money on home improvements that may turn off some buyers.

As far as ARMs are concerned, there is no stronger evidence that the slogan "When banks compete, you win" is utter baloney. Along with living in an overpriced dump that my husband and I could barely afford, the inspiration for my first book in 1991 was being stuck with a bait-and-switch "teaser rate" on our ARM that had not been disclosed to us when we took out the loan, a rate that increased significantly within a couple of years after we moved into our home. I don't remember how high the payments went, but I know that our household had to drastically cut corners, from buying our son's Christmas presents at yard sales to having to hold our own yard sale to afford plane tickets to go on vacation.

What's more, once you do get a fixed-rate loan, keep tabs on interest-rate trends. If rates move even lower, consider refinancing again to a lower rate—the rule of thumb is that if prevailing rates have moved even one percentage point lower than your current rate, it's worth it because it will make up for the "prepayment penalties" you have to incur for paying off the old mortgage or "closing costs" for the new loan—don't you love how banks figure out new and clever ways to take your money?

Next, once you have a fixed-rate loan, consider saving a bundle on mortgage interest by converting to a 15-year mortgage. Since doing so also means you're refinancing the loan, you will probably have to pay closing costs, but savings are significant with a 15-year mortgage both because it's a shorter term and because these mortgages generally feature lower rates. For example, on a $100,000 30-year mortgage, your total interest costs are $115,838, assuming a 6% interest rate. If that same mortgage were converted to a 15-year term, it would require somewhat higher monthly payments—$844 instead of $600—but you'd save a whopping $63,944 in interest payments even at the same 6% interest rate.

When it comes to home improvements, be "money-wise"—limit them to improvements that aim at a broad, not a narrow, audience. For example, you or your kids may be avid swimmers, but installing a swimming pool will turn off many buyers who aren't avid swimmers or who are just as happy to patronize the local pool and won't pay extra to "repay you" for amenities they don't want. Trust me, I speak from experience. Our second home featured an indoor Jacuzzi room and we had a heck of a time unloading the house when it was time to move. In other words, don't waste money on home improvements that force you to raise the price of your home but don't attract buyers.

In addition, try to maximize your "investment returns" on these improvements by "timing" them so that they occur at the point when you're ready to sell—hopefully right near retirement. Take kitchens, for example—scores of homeowners are forking over $50,000 or so for custom premade cabinets, granite countertops, and that "island" in the middle of the kitchen. "All of my neighbors have that stuff," you may insist. You're probably right. But you're much better off waiting to make the investment in an upgrade when you're ready to sell, when the improvement will be "in" and desirable to the next buyer, rather than forking over big bucks on an upgrade that will be out of fashion by the time you're ready to sell.

Tips for Prospective Homebuyers in Affordable Areas

What follows are some steps you should take to ensure that you find a low-cost mortgage and a high-value home.

Mortgage Tips

1. Never consider a home whose price after your down payment is more than three times your household income. Calculate what you can afford at the website of HSH Associates, a provider of mortgage information: http://www.hsh.com/calc-howmuch.html.

2. Consider only fixed-rate mortgages. Some "experts" may claim that ARMs are okay if you're only going to stay in your home for three years or less, but your home is not a disposable item like a cell phone, it's a vital part of your retirement equity. If you're only planning to live in one place for three years or less, you should rent, not buy.

3. Make a 20% down payment on the home, if possible—even if you have to borrow the money from your parents or in-laws—I wish my husband and I had done so when we bought our first home. That's because a 10% or lower down payment may mean you must purchase private mortgage insurance (PMI), which insures the bank against you

walking away from the loan—people with higher down payments are considered less risky borrowers because they have more "skin in the game." Even more important, the higher down payment also means you are more likely to be qualified for a fixed-rate mortgage.

4. Never take out an interest-only mortgage. While you pay no principal during the interest-only period, your payments will rise when that period comes to an end. What's more, the mortgage has to be paid off during a shorter term—25, 23, or 20 years—so your monthly payments will be higher.

5. Avoid one of the riskiest mortgages, a balloon loan. Talk about bait and switch: Typically, after the end of a three- or seven-year period, you owe the bank all the remaining principal, in one lump sum. If the value of your home drops you won't be able to find another mortgage to repay that loan and you risk foreclosure.

6. Never deal with a mortgage broker—deal directly with banks.

7. Get a copy of your credit history at www.annualcreditreport. com. If you have a low score due to a poor payment history (as opposed to incorrect information), I strongly urge you to postpone home ownership until you've built a better bill-payment history; doing so could literally cut your mortgage cost in half. The chart shown on page 85 shows some mind-boggling numbers: Someone with a poor score pays **almost double** in interest what someone with a great score pays.

House-Hunting Tips

Once you start house-hunting, you need to consider features that make the house a solid investment—not just ones that meet your family's needs, but will be attractive to the next buyer.

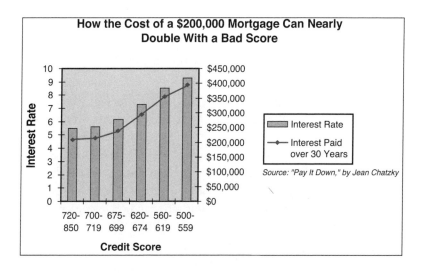

How the Cost of a $200,000 Mortgage Can Nearly Double With a Bad Score

Interest Rate

Credit Score: 720-850, 700-719, 675-699, 620-674, 560-619, 500-559

Legend: Interest Rate / Interest Paid over 30 Years

Source: "Pay It Down," by Jean Chatzky

1. First, shop around for a mortgage. Why so soon? You'll need to get preapproved by a bank for a home loan up to a certain ceiling—actually, many real estate agents will require preapproval because they don't want to waste time showing homes to potential buyers who can't afford them or won't be approved for a mortgage. **Make sure you specify that you want to be qualified for a fixed-rate mortgage.** While you're not bound to borrow from the lender and it's not obliged to offer you the loan, the lender will probably require you to pay an upfront, nonrefundable-if-you-don't-get-a-mortgage-from-them fee of a couple hundred dollars—and may also require a nonrefundable deposit too. Preapproval means you're actually starting the loan process with a lender—filling out an application, letting them go through your credit, etc.—but approval typically hinges on the property passing a satisfactory appraisal and inspection(s). That's why you should shop around for a mortgage and a lender

before you ask for a preapproval. A good place to do this is on the home page of HSH Associates under the heading: Browse Lenders and Rates in Your State: http://www.hsh.com/.

2. Once your approval is ready and you're ready to "shop," research neighborhoods by their school ranking even if you don't have or intend to have kids because the home will be more valuable to the next buyer. Typically, the state education department will have the rankings of the school district's average SAT score, the percentage of kids who go on to college, the student-teacher ratio, and other important criteria.

3. Check out how close the prospective home is to schools, along with recreation facilities: ball fields, parks, playgrounds, pools, etc. Again, these are features that may not only appeal to you but also make it a good investment for the next buyer.

4. Check out the appearance of nearby homes; you're not just investing in a home, but a neighborhood.

5. If possible, only consider homes with features that make your home a good investment for the next buyer: at least two bathrooms, a basement, three bedrooms, and a two-car garage (assuming that your prospective home is in the suburbs).

6. Consider a "bargain" home—not only fixer-uppers if you're handy with a hammer, but a small home on a large lot in a great neighborhood that can be expanded.

7. Before you make an offer on a house, "test-drive" your potential commute to work at rush hour.

8. Even if a home inspection is not required in the area where you're house-hunting, have the house inspected before you buy so that you don't wind up with expensive repairs.

Can't Afford a Home Where You Currently Live? Relocate to Your Affordable Dream House

While I can't wave a magic wand and make homes affordable in high-cost regions, those of you who are currently renting in the Northeast and California may need to consider finding a home in an affordable region that could also be a good investment because the local economy is strong. That was the subject of my first book, *The Cost-Conscious Home-Buyers' Guide*, published in 1991.

The solution to the affordability crisis now is the same as it was when I wrote that book: if you can't stand the heat, get out of the kitchen. If homes are unaffordable where you live, consider moving to where they are affordable.

For my first book I selected 20 areas within shooting distance of the national median home price at that time, $93,000. I also selected destinations that were judged to be among the 100 fastest growing between 1977 and 1987 by the forecasting firm of Data Resources Inc. in Metro Insights. Finally, I eliminated all metro areas that scored lower than 100 in the *Places Rated Almanac*'s "overall category," which took into account education, culture, climate, crime rate, and other factors in all metro areas.

As in my first book, in this chapter I am ranking locations by *Places Rated Almanac*'s ranking of "best places to live" features—because you want to look for not just a job and an affordable home but a desirable destination that will attract potential buyers of your home. To meet my criteria, the regions had to rank in the top 100 of the 379 regions nationwide.

Unfortunately, most of the regions I had picked for my first book either have become so unaffordable that they would no longer qualify or have become "riskier investments" due to the slumping

2008–2009 economy. In addition, because home prices have become ever more unaffordable, I needed a huge amount of wiggle room on home prices—more than tripling the ceiling to $300,000 because if I moved it any lower I'd lose too many top *Places Rated Almanac* rankings. Yep, that's how much home prices skyrocketed in 18 years! (All median home prices are from the National Association of Realtors.)

The six regions I chose for this book are Portland, Oregon; Denver, Colorado; San Antonio, Texas; Austin, Texas; Houston, Texas; and Raleigh, North Carolina. These regions were selected based on the following economic rankings: Moody's Economy.com, requiring that the region rank in Moody's top quintile, in the top 50 by the Milken Institute and among *Inc.* magazine's Top 20.

Moving is not for everyone and you have to consider carefully before you pull up stakes. But if you can't afford a home where you currently live, it's worth the time and effort to check out your options.

What's more, these regions may offer you the same or better amenities than you'd enjoy in your current destination. Whether it's features such as the gorgeous Columbia Gorge outside of Portland and some of the best food I've ever eaten inside of Portland; the multitude of skiing, urban trails, and white-water rafting in the Denver area; the Latino cultural events and rodeos in San Antonio; the mind-boggling array of indie rock, bluegrass, and reggae experiences in Austin; the world-class, year-round symphonies in Houston; or the museums, best-of-Broadway shows, and live concerts in Raleigh, these regions are incredible experiences *and* affordable places to live. Good luck and happy house-hunting!

Portland Median Home Price: $295,200

Why you'll want to move here:

Places Rated Almanac Overall Rating: 4
Feature Ratings—Top Grade is 100

> Ambience: 97
> Housing: 18
> Jobs: 94
> Crime: 47
> Transportation: 93
> Education: 87
> Healthcare: 68
> Recreation: 93
> Climate: 87

What you'll love about Portland: Whether it's the natural beauty, the bustling local scene, or the seasonally focused dining, Portland draws not only thousands of visitors each year but "refugees" from unaffordable regions in California and Seattle as well.

Rankings by economic experts:

> Milken: 28
> *Inc.*: 11
> Moody's: 24

What Moody's thinks: Inexpensive hydropower and mineral-free water supplies drew chip makers and other technology firms to Portland in the 1990s—and growth may continue, given that several solar panel manufacturing firms are planning to invest and hire aggressively. Over the extended horizon, Portland is expected to sustain above-average rates of growth due primarily to a continued influx of population, including an ample supply of skilled workers.

MAJOR EMPLOYERS: Intel Corporation, Providence Health Systems, Safeway Inc., Oregon Health & Science University, Fred Meyer Inc., Legacy Health System, Kaiser Permanent, Nike Inc., Portland State University, Wells Fargo Bank, U.S. Bank, Greenbrier Co's Inc., United Parcel Service Inc., Portland Community College, Southwest Washington Medical Center, McDonald's Corporation, Bonneville Power Administration, Standard Insurance Company, Farmers Insurance Company of Oregon.

CLIMATE: Summers are warm, sunny, and rather dry; winters are gray and wet, though mild.

CULTURE: <u>Summertime Concerts at Oregon Zoo:</u> featuring blues, rock, bluegrass, folk, Celtic, and jazz; <u>The Arlene Schnitzer Concert Hall,</u> home to the Oregon Symphony; <u>Jimmy Mak's;</u> <u>Berbati's Pan:</u> one of Portland's best and most popular rock clubs.

RECREATION: <u>The Japanese Garden:</u> The best time to visit is in June when the Japanese irises are in bloom; <u>Driving and Hiking on the Gorge:</u> no matter what time of year, the drive up the Columbia Gorge is spectacular; <u>Wine Tasting in the Nearby Wine Country:</u> within less than an hour's drive of Portland are dozens of wineries.

SPORTS: <u>Baseball:</u> Portland Beavers; <u>Basketball:</u> Portland Trail Blazers; <u>Auto Racing:</u> Portland International Raceway.

THINGS TO DO WITH THE KIDS: <u>The Annual Portland Pirate Festival:</u> spectacular tall ships, cannon firing, and sword-fighting demonstrations; <u>Oregon Museum of Science and Industry:</u> poke around inside the USS *Blueback;* <u>Virtual Parachuting:</u> at the World Forestry Center Discovery Museum, the kids pretend to be smoke jumpers parachuting into the woods to put out a forest fire.

Denver Median Home Price: $245,400

Why you'll want to move here:

Places Rated Almanac: 19

Ambience: 98
Housing: 26
Jobs: 99
Crime: 58
Transportation: 93
Education: 84
Healthcare: 71
Recreation: 90
Climate: 33

What you'll love about Denver: You can tell from its skyline alone that Denver is a major metropolis, with a major-league baseball stadium in the center of downtown. But look to the west to see where the Rocky Mountains, snow-peaked and breathtakingly huge, appear in the distance. People spend their weeks commuting and their weekends reveling in the multitude of skiing, camping, hiking, bicycling, and fishing areas surrounding the city limits.

Rankings by economic experts:

Milken: 44
Inc.: 20
Moody's: 10

What Moody's thinks: Denver's diversified economy and low cost of living and doing business position it for continued vigorous growth in the long run. Its popular new FasTracks light-rail construction project is designed to modernize its congested transportation infrastructure. Increased tourism would feed into a revitalized downtown and benefit airlines using Denver as a hub.

MAJOR EMPLOYERS: Quest Communication International Inc., King Soopers, HealthONE, Lockheed Martin Corp., Wal-Mart Stores, Exempla Healthcare, Safeway, Inc., University of Denver, Centura Health, United Airlines, Inc., Kaiser Permanente, Denver Health and Hospital Authority, Frontier Airlines, IBM Corporation, Dish Network, Bell Corp., United Parcel Service, Great-West Life & Annuity Insurance Company, University of Colorado Hospital, Wells Fargo Bank.

CLIMATE: Denver features a semiarid climate with typically hot summers and dry, chilly winters.

CULTURE: The Denver Art Museum; Denver March Pow-Wow: features more than 700 dancers and musicians from 70 tribes; Cinco De Mayo; Denver International Film Festival; Vans Warped Tour: leading punk and hard-core bands on 10 stages; Cherry Creek Arts Festival; Denver Botanic Gardens: more than 15,000 plant species from around the world.

RECREATION: Denver has 850 miles of urban trails, dude ranches, and fly-fishing and white-water kayaking or rafting. Winter Park Resort: offers easy access to skiers arriving at Denver International Airport; Loveland Ski Area: just 53 miles west of Denver on I-70, Loveland is the closest ski area to Denver and averages 400 inches of snow annually.

SPORTS: Baseball: The Colorado Rockies; Basketball: The Denver Nuggets; Football: The Denver Broncos; Horse Racing: Arapahoe Park; Rodeo: The National Western Stock Show, Rodeo, and Horse Show.

THINGS TO DO WITH THE KIDS: Children's Museum of Denver; Downtown Aquarium; Denver Museum of Nature & Science; Denver Zoo.

San Antonio Median Home Price: $153,200

Why you'll want to move here:

Places Rated Almanac: 24

Ambience: 83
Housing: 68
Jobs: 94
Crime: 27
Transportation: 89
Education: 75
Healthcare: 73
Recreation: 52
Climate: 77

What you'll love about San Antonio: Wake up in the Alamo City with the scent of huevos rancheros in the air, the sound of mariachis, and the sight of barges winding down the San Antonio River, and you know you're someplace special.

Rankings by economic experts:

Milken: 15
Inc.: 7
Moody's: 40

What Moody's thinks: The ongoing decline in the U.S. economy will cause San Antonio to slow. Longer term, the region's key location for international trade means that it will remain an above-average performer. The presence of a Toyota plant has positively contributed to the transportation equipment manufacturing industry. Proposed defense spending will generate additional economic activity in the metro area and help sustain viable growth in the long run.

MAJOR EMPLOYERS: Fort Sam Houston, Lackland AFB, USAA Insurance Co., Randolph AFB, The Methodist Hospital System, AT&T Corporation, Baptist Health System, University of Texas at San Antonio, Alamo Community College District, University of Texas Health Science Center at San Antonio, University Health System, CPS Energy, Wachovia Corporation, Brooke Army Medical Center, Clarke American Checks, Six Flags Fiesta Texas, Brooks Air Force Base, James A. Haley Veterans Hospital.

CLIMATE: San Antonio is hot, warm, and pleasant throughout much of the year.

CULTURE: The Alameda: The Museo Alameda uses a series of permanent and temporary exhibitions to explore the Latino experience; Fiesta Noche Del Rio; Luminaria—Arts Night in San Antonio: art, music, poetry, performance, light shows; Fiesta San Antonio; Juneteenth: picnic, festival, Freedom Fair, and cultural celebrations honoring the day Texas slaves received word of the Emancipation Proclamation.

RECREATION: Ford Holiday River Parade and Lighting Ceremony; Mitchell Lake: Bird-watchers come here to see the more than 300 species that visit each year. Natural Bridge Caverns: stalagmites, stalactites, and other wonders.

SPORTS: Basketball: San Antonio Spurs; Hockey: San Antonio Rampage; Baseball: Missions minor-league baseball.

THINGS TO DO WITH THE KIDS: The Alamo; SeaWorld San Antonio; Witte Museum: mummies and dinosaurs, Native American pictographs, fiesta gowns, and an ecolab with living Texas critters—like tarantulas.

Austin Median Home Price: $183,700

Why you'll want to move here:

Places Rated Almanac: 35

Ambience: 98
Housing: 30
Jobs: 100
Crime: 48
Transportation: 95
Education: 88
Healthcare: 32
Recreation: 52
Climate: 78

What you'll love about Austin: Whether your taste is for hip-hop, bluegrass, indie, or reggae, one of the music festival is guaranteed to rock your world. What's more, Austin is a city where you're not only allowed but expected to be yourself, in all your quirky glory. The people you encounter may even be newcomers themselves—Austin's population grew 47% during the 1990s and continues to expand at a healthy pace.

Rankings by economic experts:

Milken: 4
Inc.: 2
Moody's: 2

What Moody's thinks: The Austin—Round Rock region ranks 10th in the nation in terms of the importance of the high-tech sector to its local economy. Among high-tech industries, its highest concentration is in computer and electronic product manufacturing. Many factors will contribute to solid long-term growth. Above-average income per capita, a highly educated workforce, and the concentration of high tech will enable Austin to remain one of the top-performing metro areas in the nation.

MAJOR EMPLOYERS: Dell Inc., University of Texas at Austin, HEB Grocery Company, Seton Healthcare Network, Wal-Mart Stores, Inc., St. David's Healthcare, IBM Corp., Freescale Semiconductor Inc., Solectron Taxes, AT&T Corporation, AMC Inc., Austin Community College, Applied Materials, Texas State University-San Marcos, National Instruments, Apple Computer, Girling Health Care, Keller Williams Realty, Samsung, Austin Semiconductor, Lower Colorado River Authority.

CLIMATE: Weather in Austin is typically Texan, with hot summers and mild winters.

CULTURE: Austin City Limits Music Festival; Latino Music Month; Texas Hill Country Wine and Food Festival; Carnaval Brasileiro: combines the uninhibited sprit of Mardi Gras with colorful Brazilian flamboyance.

RECREATION: Clyde Littlefield Texas Relays; Red Eye Regatta; Star of Texas Fair & Rodeo; Capital Cruises; Republic of Texas Biker Rally; Rock Climbing: at Enchanted Rock, a stunning granite outcropping in the Hill Country; Spelunking: at Airman's Cave on the Barton Creek Greenbelt and Goat Cave Preserve in southwest Austin.

SPORTS: Baseball, Basketball, Football: University of Texas; Clyde Littlefield Texas Relays.

THINGS TO DO WITH THE KIDS: Champion Park: kids can dig for stone casts of dinosaur bones; Austin Children's Museum; Edward's Aquifer: Austin's main source of water is fed by a variety of underground creeks; Zilker Zephyr Miniature Train: take a scenic

25-minute ride through Zilker Park on a narrow-gauge, light-rail miniature train.

Houston Median Home Price: $152,500

Why you'll want to move here:

Places Rated Almanac: 48

Ambience: 84
Housing: 49
Jobs: 99
Crime: 24
Transportation: 99
Education: 63
Healthcare: 51
Recreation: 96
Climate: 39

What you'll love about Houston: With nearly 21,000 concerts, plays, exhibitions, and other arts programs presented in Houston annually, it's one of the few U.S. cities that offers world-class, year-round resident companies in all the major performing arts—symphony, opera, drama, and ballet.

Rankings by economic experts:

Milken: 16
Inc.: 4
Moody's: 50

What Moody's thinks: Opportunities stemming from the oil exploration in the Gulf have been a key engine for growth. The presence of key players in the region (namely Exxon Mobil, Shell, Chevron, and

BP) will help sustain the industry's growth. The local housing market will bottom out sooner than the nation as a whole. In the long run, even as energy prices ease, they will remain high enough to keep the region strong. It will also continue to benefit from growing space-flight development, health research, distribution, and population growth.

MAJOR EMPLOYERS: University of Texas, Wal-Mart Stores, Inc., Administaff, Memorial Hermann Healthcare System, Continental Airlines Inc., Exxon Mobil Corporation, Kroger Company, Shell Oil, the Methodist Hospital, HEB Grocery Company, Baylor College of Medicine, Hewlett-Packard Company, Baker Hughes, HCA, Chevron Corp., Harris County Hospital District, AT&T Corp., St. Luke's Episcopal Health System, BP plc, Texas Children's Hospital.

CLIMATE: Houston is home to a humid subtropical climate, featuring typically sunny Texan weather.

CULTURE: Along with the Houston Symphony and Houston Grand Opera, enjoy The Worldfest Independent Film Festival; The CaribFest Carnival, featuring reggae, zydeco, and calypso; and Theatre District Day.

RECREATION: Ballunar Liftoff Festival: The sky's the limit as more than 100 hot-air balloons majestically take off around the Johnson Space Center; Houston Hot Sauce Festival; Art Car Weekend: around 250,000 spectators converge at Houston Children's Museum to admire custom cars; The Chevron Houston Marathon: features a wheelchair race, a half-marathon, and a 5K race.

SPORTS: Baseball: Houston Astros; Basketball: Houston Rockets, Houston Comets; Hockey: Houston Aeros; Football: Houston Texans; Houston Livestock Show and Rodeo; Gulf Greyhound Park: the world's largest greyhound racing operation; <u>Houston Race Park:</u> Hosts live thoroughbred and American quarter horse racing.

THINGS TO DO WITH THE KIDS: <u>The Houston Children's Festival:</u> the festival offers more than 350 events packed into a couple of days; <u>Downtown Aquarium;</u> <u>SplashTown:</u> take the plunge and then some at this extreme water park located north of the city; <u>Kemah Boardwalk:</u> climb aboard the Boardwalk Bullet, a wooden roller coaster, and ride the Ferris wheel, The Red Train, and nine other amusement rides; <u>Houston Zoo.</u>

Raleigh Median Home Price: $224,200

Why you'll want to move here:

Places Rated Almanac: 57

> Ambience: 93
> Housing: 39
> Jobs: 96
> Crime: 37
> Transportation: 71
> Education: 89
> Healthcare: 44
> Recreation: 70
> Climate: 50

What you'll love about Raleigh: Raleigh is Old South and New South, down-home and upscale. The city has agrarian roots but thrives on high-tech industries, government (it's the state capital), education, service industries, research, and medicine. Best known for its world-class museums, best of Broadway shows, and live concerts, Greater Raleigh offers a variety of entertainment all in one parklike, scenic setting. No fewer than six college campuses dot the city's streets, with wide lawns and impressive brick buildings.

Rankings by economic experts:

Milken: 2
Inc.: 1
Moody's: 3

What Moody's thinks: The long-term outlook is for Raleigh to perform well above average as the Research Triangle attracts more new firms in established industries and also as it continues to become more diverse.

Major employers: Duke University Hospital, North Carolina State University, WakeMed Health and Hospitals, Pinkerton & Burns, Rex Healthcare, SAS Institute, WakeMed Faculty Physicians, Cisco Systems, Waste Energies Inc., Progress Energy, Verizon Communications, Eaton Division, Food Lion Stores.

CLIMATE: Raleigh features a moderate, continental climate.

CULTURE: North Carolina Symphony; The Opera Company of North Carolina; North Carolina Museum of History; North Carolina Museum of Art; Full Frame Documentary Festival; International Festival; Time Warner Cable Music Pavilion at Walnut Creek: attracts whoever is topping the pop and country charts; Artsplosure: celebrates excellence in the performing and visual arts by bringing together national, regional, and local artists.

RECREATION: William B. Umstead State Park: offers 20 miles of hiking trails, boat rentals, and mountain bike trails; Capital City Bicycle Motocross Race Track: open to the public and organized according to age groups and skill levels; <u>Cedar Hills Park Disc Golf Course</u>; <u>Fantasy Lake Scuba Park</u>; <u>Falls Lake State Recreation Area</u>.

SPORTS: <u>Hockey</u>: Carolina Hurricanes; <u>Baseball</u>: Carolina Mudcats; <u>Wake County Speedway</u>; <u>PGA Golf Tournaments</u>.

THINGS TO DO WITH THE KIDS: <u>Silver Lake Water Park</u>; <u>North Carolina Museum of Natural Sciences</u>; <u>Pullen Aquatic Center</u>; <u>Adventure Landing</u>: three miniature golf courses, speedway go-karts, extreme laser tag, and more.

PART III

College Is Unaffordable When the Majority of Americans Need Degrees

Chapter 6

Why We Need More College Graduates to Compete with China and India

Why do we care about the price of getting a sheepskin? Two reasons: First, a college degree is a necessary investment in getting your kids a well-paying job at a point in history when increasing numbers of working-class jobs are being outsourced. Second, the less money you have to fork over for your kids' degrees means the more you can bankroll for your retirement.

How fast have college costs risen? If our current President had lacked the talent to author two bestsellers, he'd probably still be paying off his college bills, since he opted to use his law degree, which he got in 1988, to enter public service rather than a more lucrative career as a trial lawyer. The Obamas often say they would still be in debt if not for royalties from his books, which began to swell the couple's bank account in 2005. For some time, the couple's college loan payments were higher than their monthly mortgage payments, Michelle Obama would tell audiences on the campaign trail.

In 1958, the annual tuition at Northwestern University was about 16% of a typical family income, and it took less than 57 days of pay to foot the bill. In 2003 it consumed more than 53% of a year's income—and that same household would have to work almost 195 days to pay it off.

A generation ago, Americans weren't obligated to foot most of the cost of their tuition, or their kids' tuition; while federal grants accounted for 70% of the cost of a degree 30 years ago, loans now account for 64% of the cost.

How did the cost of a four-year degree morph from manageable to through-the-roof? As is the case with U.S. home prices, shrinking federal subsidies. Former President Ronald Reagan, who ran for governor of California on a promise to crack down on the "freaks, brats, and cowardly fascists" who made up the student protestors at UC Berkeley, continued his vendetta against the government subsidy of "intellectual curiosity" while campaigning for president. Although he was not able to follow through on his proposal to abolish the U.S. Department of Education once he was elected President, he did halve the portion of the federal budget spent on education from 12% of the budget to 6%.

In the same fashion that most of the developed world's pension systems and Canada's banking system puts America's version of both to shame, for the most developed country in the world, we are one of the most frugal when it comes to subsidizing higher education. Currently most governments around the world take primary responsibility for the financing of higher education.

Of the 30 OECD countries, the U.S. is the third-lowest spender; only Japan and Korea spend less. Government subsidies in the U.S. account for only around 40% of the total cost of getting a diploma, compared to more than 80% of it in Greece, Denmark, Norway, Poland, Turkey, Austria, Portugal, Belgium, Sweden, Iceland, Ireland, Germany, the Slovak Republic, and France—tuition is actually free in France. Even some poor countries spend more than we do: public expenditure as a portion of the total is 60% or more in Argentina, Thailand, and Jamaica.

Perhaps the commitment of other governments to higher education is the reason why a higher percentage of overseas students are graduating. While 20 years ago the U.S. was first among industrialized nations when it comes to college participation rates, we're no longer even in the top 10, according to the OECD. As a result, our share of the world's population of college students has fallen from 30% 30 years ago to 14% and is continuing to fall because our global competition is racing us to the top, according to the National Center for Education and the Economy (NCEE).

This challenge is not lost on President Obama and he has alerted Americans to the fact that a high-school diploma alone will no longer cut the mustard. In an address to a Joint Session of Congress in late February of 2009, he said, "I ask every American to commit to at least one year or more of higher education or career training. This can be community college or a four-year school; vocational training or an apprenticeship. But whatever the training may be, every American will need to get more than a high school diploma. Let's meet a new goal; by 2020, America will once again have the highest proportion of college graduates in the world."

Sounds like a plan, Mr. President. Next, let's make sure Americans will no longer pay through the nose to attain this goal. A poll of likely voters commissioned by the National Education Association and released two months before the presidential election showed that 70% of parents and 65% of students said making college affordable was an important issue for them in the election. In May 2007, polling by Public Agenda for the National Center for Public Policy and Higher Education says that 62% of Americans believe that many well-qualified students do not have an opportunity to get a higher education, the highest proportion since polling began in 1993.

Now More Than Ever, a College Degree Is Needed to Succeed

As we enter the 21st century, we face the tough challenge that the country that has led the free world for the past century no longer holds the patent on prosperity. Because the U.S. is faced with wage competition from a worldwide market of low-cost labor, going to college isn't simply an opportunity to do better than your parents but a necessity for many to survive.

Too many on Capitol Hill need to wake up to the fact that the task before us isn't for one political party's ideology to prevail over that of the other, but to create a bipartisan dialogue on putting America back on track to compete against other countries for high-paying jobs. Maybe we need to frame the challenge as a "global economic Olympics."

If, as the NCEE says, the U.S. will need to be number one or two in technology leadership in every industry in which we expect to be a major competitor, we need to send everyone, or almost everyone, to college.

America's "shrinking blue collar" is evidenced by the precipitous drop in manufacturing jobs; In January of 2009, 207,000 of these jobs vanished, in the largest one-month drop in 27 years. While the U.S. is still the world's leading manufacturer by value, hitting a record $1.6 trillion in 2007, we require fewer workers to make what other people buy. While 28% of U.S. workers held manufacturing jobs 50 years ago, only 8% do today.

And it's not just the outsourcing of manufacturing jobs but the "automation" of many clerical and blue-collar jobs that threatens middle-class living standards. Up until the 1980s or so, companies needed secretaries and clerks to type up memos and letters; now most people compose, edit, and e-mail their own—it's amazing that the U.S. Post Office is still in business, given the wireless world's domination of communication. In addition, ATM cards have downsized the bank-teller field, and scanners at checkout counters have affected the jobs of checkout clerks.

If you need evidence that outsourcing poses a threat to America's middle-class jobs, witness the exponential growth of India's and China's middle class. Research by the World Bank shows that in just 15 years, between 1990 and 2005, India's middle class rose by 55%, from 147 million people to 264 million. In China the numbers are even more staggering, rising more than 400% from 174 million to 806 million.

The rise of the middle class in China and India is one important reason why $150-a-barrel oil prices didn't cause the Consumer Price Index to go bananas in 2009, as was the case three decades ago—especially in 1973 and 1979—a trend that doesn't appear to have registered on the minds of any of the Fed chairmen, who are constantly agonizing about inflation. This isn't the 1970s, when inflation was assisted by rising wages enabled by the clout of labor unions; many Americans got cost of living allowances and retailers responded by raising prices. That won't happen now because as *Newsweek* International Editor Fareed Zakaria puts it, one way to think about India and China is as two great global *deflation machines* (italics mine), pumping out goods (China) and services (India) for a fraction of what they would cost to produce in the West.

Very likely because the U.S. media does a poor job of covering the meteoric rise of India and China's economies and their effect on ours former Iowa governor (and current Secretary of Agriculture) Tom Vilsack recalls the culture shock he experienced on a 1999 trip to Shanghai and his resulting worries about the U.S. "Before I went, I had this image of China as being somewhat backward," he says, "and I went to this city that had more skyscrapers than I had ever seen in my life. I don't think people understand this is what China is going to be."

Said Vilsack, to compete with China, India, and other emerging economic powers, the U.S. needs a better-educated workforce. His message in Iowa was that schools have to teach more math and science and that parents have to wake up and realize that in a 21st century world, their kids aren't just competing against the neighboring town's baseball team but against their peers in China and India.

"Parents say, 'I don't want Johnny to take calculus because it is going to ruin his grade-point average,'" Vilsack continued. 'I don't want Susie to take physics because she has got softball practice and it's going to require her to take lab.' What these parents need for someone to say is, 'If you want the next generation to have it better than you, you are going to have to convince the kids to take math and science and get excited about it because that's where the future is.'"

Not only do Johnny and Susie need to take calculus, but their teachers need to do a better job teaching it: the test scores of American students were the fifth lowest of the 30 countries ranked by the National Governors Association in 2006.

Perhaps we need to reframe our No Child Left Behind education reform efforts as "Aiming to Stay Ahead of, or at Least Keep Up with, India and China." In fact, the reason China and India's economies are racing us to the top may have to do with their educational systems. In 1949, when India gained its independence, Jawaharlal Nehru, its first prime minister, commissioned the creation of elite technological colleges called the Indian Institutes of Technology. One of the reasons why many Indians are able to seek graduate degrees at our top universities is because of the rigorous standards in math, science, and English at these institutes, which in turn caused the elementary and secondary schools to raise their standards. Teachers at secondary schools in India expect many of their students to be absent from school for not less than a quarter of their regular classes during their last year of classes to prepare for these exams; parents typically suspend social activities to help them.

The story in China is similar. When Deng Xiaoping became premier after the death of Mao Zedong in the late 1970s, he saw that China's future depended heavily on excellence in research and teaching at its leading universities, particularly in engineering. Shortly after coming to power, he set a goal of creating 100 research universities and 20 world-class research parks.

We Need Universities to Shake Their Money Trees

The irony is that in some cases the solution to the U.S. college afford-ability crisis isn't to shift the funding responsibility back to the feder-al government; many private colleges themselves could replace loans with grants. A record 76 colleges and universities reached endow-ments of $1 billion or more in 2007; what's most outrageous is that many of these colleges have doubled their price of admission over the past decade—despite tripling their wealth over that same period.

The assets of Harvard's endowment, at one point as high as $34.6 billion, was almost as large as that of the nation's largest charitable foundation: The Bill & Melinda Gates Foundation. For $300 million, less than 1% of its endowment, Harvard could offer a free ride to its students rather than charging them $188,000 apiece.

In February of 2008, the Senate Finance Committee asked 136 colleges with endowments of $500 million or more for detailed infor-mation on their financial aid spending. Embarrassed by public scruti-ny of their lack of largesse, more than 60 name-brand colleges have already launched their own spend-down initiatives, including replac-ing loans with grants to students with household incomes that fall below a certain ceiling.

Some examples: Harvard now allows families earning $120,000 to $180,000 a year to limit tuition obligations to 10% of their income, Williams College announced it will replace loans with grants in 2009, and Wesleyan will substitute grants for loans for students from families with less than $40,000 in income. (A link to the complete list of the col-leges is in Chapter 8, "The Fix: Grants, Government Loans, and Colleges That Are Free.")

College Grants Favor Rich Applicants Who Will "Repay" Them over the Truly Needy

If President and Mrs. Obama received any scholarships for their undergraduate degrees, they were in the minority. Just 8.1% of Harvard's 9,500 undergrads get Pell Grants, which are awarded to families with less than $50,000 in income—what's more, the measly average grant award of $2,400 per year would help few, if any, prospective students afford to get a degree. A recent study of students at 19 elite colleges found that only 6% were the first in their families to attend college and only 11% were from families with incomes of $35,000 or less. These colleges aren't just elite, they're elitist.

The "inconvenient truth" about college endowments isn't just that colleges aren't using a larger percentage of them to help students, it's that historically the students they have helped the most are not the deserving poor but the affluent—who are likely to "return the favor" by boosting their alma mater's endowments as alumni, not to mention boosting its rankings with *US News & World Report*. To put it another way, when these colleges have a choice between giving a bright, poor kid a free ride and five rich, smart kids a subsidized ride, they have a financial incentive to choose the latter.

For the most part, the only poor kids who are likely to get a full scholarship are the ones who apply to second-tier institutions that need to boost their standings in the rankings. For example, a friend of my daughter's is a top-notch student (1600 SAT scores) from a poor family who was offered *partial* scholarships to Yale and Harvard but a full scholarship to Boston University. The folks at Yale and Harvard had to know that the cash-strapped student would have to turn them down, so the gesture could have been largely symbolic, making them *appear* to be generous. Why did BU offer a free ride? Because BU is ranked lower than Yale or Harvard by *US News & World Report*, the student's 1600 SAT scores would boost its ranking. Why didn't Yale and Harvard offer him a free ride? As I mentioned before, they'd rather help a rich kid who will more likely be a rich alumni who will fatten their coffers—plus, being Yale and Harvard, they don't need any help boosting their rankings.

Colleges Don't Compete for Our Bucks Because We Think Price = Quality

Incredibly, along with ranking colleges based on the IQs of the kids going there, *US News & World Report* puts a high ranking on the salaries of their professors and how rich their alumni are by alumni giving. Says author Richard Vedder in his book *Going Broke by Degree*, "When federal legislation was approved in the late 1990s offering tuition tax credits, I jokingly referred to it as the Faculty Salary Enhancement Act, reasoning that for every $1,000 in tuition tax credit granted, universities would raise their tuition by close to $1,000."

Colleges don't compete for your business by lowering their costs like regular businesses do. Vedder observes that while American businesses restructured and downsized to become leaner and meaner in the late 1980s and 1990s, you rarely heard of a university doing the same—for example, dropping a course of studies because of decreased enrollment or decreased relevance, or getting rid of tenure. On the contrary, deans and department chairs are always trying to increase their budget, since bigger budgets mean more power. Vedder also theorizes that colleges can get away with jacking up tuition because parents complain to their congresspeople, not the colleges, and Congress reacts by boosting subsidies.

In the next chapter, we'll look at detailed action steps you can take to get Congress to lower college costs, and Chapter 8 offers tips on shopping for an affordable degree.

Chapter 7

How Sallie Mae Lobbied Congress and "Enticed" Colleges to Offer Its Loans

Just as the mortgage industry managed to make homes more expensive through the use of expensive mortgages such as ARMs and interest-only loans, Sallie Mae, the dominant lender in the student-loan market, has made college more expensive by lobbying for interest-rate subsidies, and by attempting to elbow the low-cost federal government lending program out of the market.

It also profits by its ability to collect debt in just about any circumstance—whether or not the graduate can repay the loan. In a 2006 *60 Minutes* piece on Sallie Mae, Lesley Stahl interviewed Alan Michael Collinge, who graduated with degrees in aerospace engineering in 1998 but had a tough time finding a job that would enable him to repay his debt. In 2001 he asked Sallie Mae for a payment forbearance (lengthening the terms of the loan), but the lender refused and instead placed Collinge's loan into default. Thanks to the corrosive effect of compound interest in reverse, his debt for a loan of about $38,000 more than doubled by 2005 to about $103,000.

In and out of work, Collinge struggled after he got his degree. When he finally defaulted, his loan was turned over to a guarantor, an agency that takes over a student loan in default but still attempts to collect the loan from the borrower—in this case Sallie Mae was both the lender and the guarantor. While credit card companies will often negotiate the debt repayment, Sallie Mae refused. Ironically enough, it's precisely because his inability to repay the loan damaged his credit rating that he didn't get the security clearance that would lead to a high-paying job as an aerospace engineer that would enable him to repay it. "It would be very tough for me to get anything but the lowest level of security clearance with my credit record destroyed as it is," Collinge said.

While even the powerful credit card industry can't get past bankruptcy to garnish what's left of the cardholder's assets, if a student falls on very hard times after graduation and has to go bankrupt, federal law says bankruptcy doesn't affect the collection of student loans. The student lending industry can even get to a debtor's disability insurance payments under Social Security. It gets worse. Guess who owns some of the largest collection agencies? You guessed it—Sallie Mae. When its collection agency collects, it gets 25% of the recovery.

Sadly enough, if Collinge had gone to college in England, he wouldn't be in this pickle. For one thing, college is cheaper: you can pay as little as $36,000 for a degree—yes, you read it right—as opposed to $20,000 to $50,000 a year. What's more, British students who take out loans don't have to repay them until they get full-time jobs and they are earning at least £15,000 a year. So if they end up with a job that doesn't pay well or never land a job, they owe nothing. About half of the students in England either pay nothing for their degree or pay for only a portion of it.

A $40 Million Paycheck to Make Expensive Loans

Contrast Collinge's financial fate to that of former Sallie Mae CEO, Albert L. Lord (he is currently vice chairman). A 2004 article in *The Washington Post* reported that Lord got $41.8 million in total compensation that year and president Thomas Fitzpatrick got $27.8 million, ranking them second and fourth, respectively, in the *Post's* survey of executive compensation in the region.

When you make $40 million a year or so, you don't just go to baseball games and play golf for fun. You try to buy baseball teams, and you actually do buy land on which to build a golf course. In 2005, Lord tried to buy the Washington Nationals baseball team, with a price tag of $450 million. While the outcome of the baseball deal wasn't clear, Lord did end up paying $4.2 million, about $17,000 an acre, for several acres of land on which he planned to build a golf course for his own amusement.

What's ridiculous about an obscene paycheck for a student loan executive is that it's a business that doesn't even need to exist—there is a much cheaper alternative: the direct lending program by the federal government. If we can't shift more of the burden of paying for college to other sources, the least we can do is let Sallie Mae and other private lenders go out of business, a goal that many Democrats on Capitol Hill want to accomplish but haven't to date due to Sallie Mae's lobbying efforts. In other countries, governments subsidize more of the cost of college as the U.S. used to do before the Reagan Administration; the least we can do is lower the cost of college debt. We don't force our students or their parents to pay for the cost of a vitally needed elementary, middle, or high-school education. Why should we expect our citizens to foot most or all of the bill's cost for higher education—in fact, increasing the bill because of interest paid on the debt?

How Sallie Mae Came to Dominate the Market

Starting in the mid-1960s, the federal government provided insurance to reimburse lenders for 99% of the loan value in the event of a default to encourage banks to lend to college students, who were considered risky borrowers because they typically had little credit history and no collateral or predicable income. The government also agreed to guarantee the lenders a certain level of profit as long as they adhered to an interest-rate cap. The loans in question, established in 1980, are guaranteed by the government at 9.5%.

When the government established Sallie Mae in 1972, a special charter allowed it to use low-cost debt, backed by the Feds, to buy existing student loans from banks. It pocketed the difference between the cost of the funds and the interest payments the students made. But as a Government Sponsored Enterprise (GSE), it was barred from lending directly to students. Sallie Mae's purpose was to create a secondary market for the loans, like Fannie Mae and Freddie Mac do for mortgages. As a GSE, they could borrow funds at close to government interest rates and buy loans that were guaranteed. At the same time, the company was owned by private stockholders.

While the government's direct lending program has been in existence since 1965, President Clinton was responsible for elevating it from a pilot program to a full program as part of the Student Loan Reform Act of 1993, hoping to have direct lending from the government and capture 60% of the market over six years. As a result, Sallie Mae's stock, as high as $73 in 1993, began to fall. Then Congress hobbled Sallie Mae by slapping a 30-basis-point fee (a basis point is one-hundredth of a percentage point) on all its new loans.

Unfortunately, when you only fix part of the problem with student loans, you worsen the problem. Sallie Mae's reaction to the fact that it was losing business as a result of direct lending by the government was to enter the lending business and "entice" colleges to steer students to its loans. In 1997, Sallie Mae's new management team severed its government ties, allowing it to lend directly to students for the first time. As it snapped up smaller rivals, Sallie Mae quickly became the industry's biggest player. Today it originates nearly 23% of all loans and carries about $142 billion, or 29% of all loans, on its books.

Compromising on Good Legislation = Bad Legislation

One of the reasons "change" is going to be a challenge for President Obama is that as soon as a President or brave Congressperson thinks up good legislation, the business lobby may threaten members of Congress with a withdrawal of campaign contributions unless they add amendments that create bad legislation. When Congress tightened the bankruptcy treatment of student loans in 1998, Clinton wanted a reduction in student-loan interest rates, which lenders opposed. So Clinton got what he wanted—lower interest rates—in exchange for lenders getting what they wanted—the ability to collect student-loan debt regardless of the student's ability to pay.

In 2000, Congress created the misleadingly named "opportunity loans," in which Sallie Mae "incentivises" colleges to leave the low-cost government-sponsored direct loan program. In effect, Sallie Mae sets up the universities as temporary banks, and the schools are guaranteed profits on the loans. As a result of this move, according to *U.S. News & World Report*, in 2003 a total of 62 colleges dropped out of the direct loan program—something that most likely isn't communicated to students when they apply to these colleges.

Then, in 2002, Sallie Mae got Congress to eliminate a planned interest-rate reduction that would have reduced student borrower debt. That change may cost taxpayers $8 billion by 2011, since we subsidize those interest rates—a fairly outrageous obligation, given the profitability of the student-loan industry.

Rep. John Boehner's Trusted Hands

As former chairman of the House Education and Labor Committee (he is now House Minority Leader), Rep. John Boehner (R-OH) offered assurances that he would protect private lenders' interests. On several occasions Boehner was a guest of Lord, Sallie Mae's CEO from 1997 to 2005 and subsequently vice chairman of its board, on the company's corporate jet, primarily for golf outings in Florida.

Loan-industry officials succeeded in getting Boehner to draft legislation that changed the federal loan-consolidation program, which allows borrowers to combine and refinance their federal student loans. The industry sought to end the ability for borrowers to lock in a low fixed interest rate for up to 30 years, as they can now. Also at Boehner's urging, the legislation would make it more difficult to extend the time borrowers have to make their payments without refinancing their loans.

Boehner also succeeded in getting a provision into the bill that would allow lawmakers to determine how much the Education Department could spend each year to administer its student-aid programs. Direct lending would have to compete each year with other legislative priorities.

Unlike most politicians, who at least attempt to pretend they put taxpayers' interests over those of big business, Boehner made no bones about where his priorities lay. In a speech delivered in December of 2005 before the Consumer Bankers Association, Boehner sought to reassure lenders that they would be happy with the final legislation. "Know that I have all of you in my two trusted hands...I've got enough rabbits up my sleeve to get where we need to."

At least one of Boehner's former colleagues observed that he puts the interests of the lending industry over those of his constituents. "The problem John faces is that he's so close to K Street," former

Rep. Christopher Shays, a Connecticut Republican, told Bloomberg.com in 2006, referring to the street in Washington, D.C., where most lobbyists have their headquarters.

Sallie Mae's College Coziness

Perhaps the most insidious practice by Sallie Mae and other lenders is using their clout at colleges—essentially getting many of them to steer students to their loans.

In 2007, it was reported that Nelnet, a student lender, paid about $1 million to two college alumni groups in exchange for exclusive referrals, according to a Senate report released by Sen. Edward Kennedy (D-MA).

In April of 2007 Sallie Mae accepted a $2 million settlement with New York State's Attorney General Andrew Cuomo and agreed to end the practice of offering opportunity loans. Yet moments after Cuomo announced the agreement at a news conference, Thomas Fitzpatrick, Sallie Mae's CEO at the time, brazenly issued a letter to colleges promising that the company would find a way to keep writing them.

Sallie Mae also said it would end the practice of sending its staff to work for free in financial offices or operating call centers at 20 colleges where company employees provided financial advice but identified themselves only as university advisers. The deal was hailed as effectively creating a national set of guidelines designed to limit conflicts of interest that could prevent students from getting objective financial advice from their schools.

Or does it? At least one student borrower advocate doesn't think so. Luke Swarthout, formerly with United States Public Interest Research Group, or U.S. PIRG, and now a consultant, stated, "This is a Band-Aid when we really need congressional reform that gets at the disease. The oversight of the federal student-loan program is coming out of Albany, New York. Which raises the question: where is Washington, D.C. on this issue?"

Even more unsettling is that the college administrators permitted this practice to happen—let's face it, when it comes to corruption, "it takes two to tango." It gets worse. Along with being compensated to steer students to Sallie Mae's expensive loans, college administrators will also accept paybacks for steering students to study-abroad programs for a semester.

I remember sitting in the audience of a meeting of parents of prospective college students at a pricey university in 2006 and listening to one of the admissions administrators rhapsodizing about the merits of studying abroad for a semester. "Let me get this straight," I thought to myself. "We'd already be paying a fortune—$40,000 a year—for her degree if she gets into this place. And even more so that she could learn how to party in a different language for a semester?"

While the "payback" of a semester abroad to students is questionable, in my opinion, unless the student is a language major, there's a strong possibility that the speaker in question or her colleagues were getting a payback. At many campuses, the companies running study-abroad programs offer colleges generous perks to sign up students: free or subsidized travel abroad and even cash bonuses and commissions on student-paid fees. For example, the American Institute for Foreign Study (AIFS) offers college officials a free trip to one of its overseas sites for every 15 students who sign on, and a 5% share of the fees that students pay. (While an official from AIFS said that the payments were "typically used for scholarships and/or support services," there wasn't any requirement to do so.)

This monetary incentive is probably the explanation for the 150% increase in enrollment of students studying abroad over the past decade, not an increased interest in honing foreign-language skills.

How Sallie Mae Courts the Vote

Albert Lord also found ways to use Sallie Mae's campaign contributions to create fake grass-roots efforts to maintain its market share. In February of 2007, Representatives George Miller (D-CA) and Barney Frank sent letters to Lord, the White House, and the Education Department seeking records of their communications since November 2006. The records, labeled "Federal Government Relations Strategy Discussion," detailed that the lender planned to make campaign contributions to members of the Congressional Black and Congressional Hispanic Caucuses and hoped to persuade Michael Lomax, president of the United Negro College Fund, to write a letter to the nation's historically black colleges and universities urging them to resist the proposed cuts in interest-rate subsidies.

Lord also lost money for his shareholders—and ultimately taxpayers—by taking irresponsible risks. Sallie Mae lost $1.64 billion in the fourth quarter of 2007, compared to a profit of $18 million in the comparable quarter a year earlier. "Sallie Mae has lent too much money to students who have gone to schools without very good graduation records," was Lord's explanation.

In January of 2008, soon after being named One of the Worst CEOs of the Year by *The Wall Street Journal* columnist Herb Greenberg, Lord reached a settlement over its scuttled $25 billion buyout by JPMorgan Chase, Bank of America, and others. The deal fell through because of adverse changes to the company's outlook as a result of the College Cost Reduction and Access Act of 2007 and the tightening of the global credit market following the 2007 subprime mortgage mess.

Unfortunately, every time Congress has the guts to pass good legislation, such as the College Cost Reduction and Access Act of 2007, which would cut subsidies on government-backed private loans, Sallie Mae or its counterparts lobby for bad legislation to bail them out. After dozens of lenders exited the business and the industry pleaded for relief, Congress passed legislation in 2008 that paved the way for the administration to intervene with "offers of temporary federal support [that] insure lenders have the incentives, and, if necessary, the liquidity needed" to stay in business, according to then-Secretary of Education Margaret Spellings.

What's baffling about the response by members of Congress to the pleas by lenders is that it occurred before the credit crunch and the economic downturn. There is no evidence that the banks needed help—and even if they were struggling, it's because they made bad business decisions, in which case they deserved to go out of business. For some reason, our political leadership believes that companies that make bad judgments should go on tax-payer-funded welfare— presumably because they are Too Big to Fail--whether they are in the business of making mortgage loans, college loans, or cars. This is especially outrageous given the fact that the student-loan industry has developed protections that enable it to collect student debt in virtually any circumstance.

A spokeswoman for Senator Kennedy insists that his goal is to have direct lending take over. Said Melissa Wagoner, "In the long term, Senator Kennedy believes that the best and most reliable option for students is for colleges to remove banks and lenders from the equation and use the Education Department's Direct Loan Program instead."

It sounds like a plan, Senator. The challenge will be finding the support from your colleagues, too many of whom prize campaign contributions from student lenders over the priorities of their constituents.

Congress and President Obama Take Steps in the Right Direction

Along with credit card reform, education is one area where Congress has tried to do right on behalf of its citizens, largely thanks to the leadership of Senator Kennedy and Representative Miller; the latter became chairman of the House Education and Labor Committee when the Democrats took control of Congress. Miller authored the College Cost Reduction and Access Act, which was signed into law by President Bush in September of 2007, which boosts the student Pell Grant program by $11.4 billion, halves the interest rate on government-subsidized student loans, and offers loan forgiveness to graduates who go into public service for at least 10 years.

Then, in August of 2008, Congress took a fairly bold step and overwhelmingly approved a measure that would require colleges with the largest tuition increases to tell the Department of Education why the increases were needed and what they will do to keep costs down in the future. The measure also requires colleges to disclose all relationships with student lenders and bans all gifts and revenue-sharing agreements between institutions and lenders offering private loans—which should theoretically put Sallie Mae and other lenders out of business.

Along with wanting more kids to go to college, the even better—and not surprising—news is that President Obama is committed to getting private lenders out of the business and boosting Pell Grants. In February of 2009, he outlined a vast overhaul of the system, aiming to end years of federal support to banks and other lenders, effective in 2010. Then in March of 2009, he announced a plan to raise the maximum Pell Grant to $5,550 a year, indexing it to inflation.

Solution to the College Cost Crisis: Shift Costs Away from Households onto Rich Taxpayers, the Colleges, and Their Rich Alumni

A college education should be a taxpayer-subsidized right for low- and middle-income Americans, not a privilege whose borrowing costs are profitable to banks. We should commend Representative Miller and President Obama for their efforts and hope that Congress will go a step further. As far as wealthy colleges with huge endowments are concerned, given that the harsh glare of publicity has already "shamed" some institutions into changing their tuition subsidy practices, for the most part annual rankings of colleges on their level of generosity will compel most of them to change—what's more, those institutions with a high ranking might use it to "compete" for the best students.

However, as for the majority of colleges that don't have multimillion dollar endowments, we need to increase the share of college costs that are subsidized by federal grants so that rich taxpayers are subsidizing the cost rather than endowing colleges with buildings that are named after them. Here are six recommended reform measures to lower college costs, and here is the email address for Rep. Miller, your go-to guy on college reform: http://georgemiller.house.gov/contactus/2007/08post_1.html.

1. Increase Pell Grants so that they cover 70% of college costs, as they did before the Reagan Administration. The President's plan to only raise the annual limits to $5,500, indexed to inflation, still forces most students or their parents to foot most of the bill for a diploma, given that the cost of college ranges from $20,000 to $50,000 a year.

2. If it's not possible to increase tuition subsidies because of budget shortfalls, consider reversing the shortfall by reinstating the pre-Reagan tax rates on high-income earners; the top marginal rate was 70% when he took office and is 35%

now. In virtually every other country in the developed world, the wealthy subsidize higher education for the poor.

3. While the new 2008 law reining in Sallie Mae bans revenue sharing, somehow I feel that Sallie Mae will figure out new and clever ways to continue to push its opportunity loans. Until we get rid of these loans, we should promote strategies for encouraging prospective college students to "boycott" any college that only offers opportunity loans. Any college that chooses to substitute them for the government's direct lending program should be required to report this move to the Department of Education, which should publish the names on its website so that prospective students can avoid applying to these colleges.

4. While it's good that Congress is shedding a harsh light on rising sticker prices, I'm more concerned about raising the level of disadvantaged students who are accepted. The U.S. Department of Education should publish an annual College Scholarship Hall of Fame and Shame, a ranking of the percentage of endowments allocated to tuition subsidies along with the percentage of its students whose family incomes are $60,000 or less (adjusted for inflation). The goal: No family earning $60,000 or less should have to pay anything for college.

5. Remove the tax-deductibility feature for any donations to a university other than those that subsidize student tuition by providing scholarships. Wealthy alumni must realize that subsidizing tuition for poor students is more important than endowing a building. (We'll let them name the scholarships after themselves.) We need more rich alumni to follow the path of Sydney Frank, who made millions marketing Jagermeister and other alcohol brands, and gave a whopping $100 million to Brown University in 2004 for the sole purpose of helping poor kids get scholarships. Frank's motivation to do so wasn't to "reward" Brown for the influence it

had on his career success—he left Brown after one year in the late 1930s because he couldn't afford to stay. More likely, he did so because it was the right thing to do.

6. Enact former Sen. Hillary Clinton's Student Borrower Bill of Rights, which includes the right to discharge debt in the event of a bankruptcy and to refinance interest rates, along with putting caps on student-loan interest rates.

Campaign Contributions That Will Challenge Reform

Americans may assume that a Democratic majority in Congress and a President who is passionate about education reform will make reform more likely. It's certainly true that better ideas will come out of the Health Education and Labor Committee now that a man of integrity is running it, Rep. George Miller, rather than John Boehner, who put K Street's priorities over those of the electorate. However, Democratic members of Congress are equally compromised by campaign contributions. Thirty-seven of the 48 members of the current committee received more than $565,000 in contributions from the top 20 student lenders in the 2007–2008 election cycle alone, including 21 Democrats, according to the Center for Responsive Politics.

Chapter 8

The Fix: Grants, Government Loans, and Colleges That Are Free

My Dad, who normally didn't mind spending money, was appalled when I was accepted to Syracuse University in 1966 because the bill would be a whopping $3,000 a year—compared to about $50,000 now! He was annoyed that he had to take out a home equity loan to pay for my brother's and my education—probably because scholarships paid for a big chunk of my Dad's bill at the University of Toronto, where he went to college when his family moved back to Canada. But at least Dad made a decent enough salary as a pension actuary to afford to repay the loan for my education. If I had to depend on my salary as a journalist to repay a student loan, I'd probably still be paying the debt 20 years later, as were President and Mrs. Obama until the royalties from his books started rolling in. Compare my fate to that of Alan Michael Collinge (the student described in Chapter 7, "How Sallie Mae Lobbied Congress and 'Enticed' Colleges to Offer Its Loans"), who was hounded by creditors when he couldn't pay his debts either because he couldn't find a job or because the job he found didn't pay enough for him to repay the loan.

After struggling with seven-day-a-week jobs to repay his debt, Collinge decided he wouldn't simply "get mad," he'd "get even" and wound up starting a political action committee called StudentLoanJustice.org in March of 2005. What started out as just a website broadened into a grass-roots effort to push for student-loan reform. Momentum increased when Bethany McLean, the reporter who first broke the Enron story, wrote an article in *Fortune* in December of 2005 describing the lobbying efforts of Sallie Mae. Then in May 2006, *60 Minutes* ran the program on Sallie Mae featuring StudentLoanJustice.org members.

A week after the *60 Minutes* piece ran, StudentLoanJustice.org was asked to have a teleconference with then-Sen. Hillary Clinton's education staff. The result: the Student Borrower Bill of Rights was introduced into the Senate on May of 2006, giving the borrowers bankruptcy rights, refinancing rights, and payment caps. Then, Sen. Dick Durbin (D-IL) introduced a bill in June 2007 to restore full bankruptcy protection for borrowers taking out private student loans. Unfortunately, because convincing a legislator to draft a bill is one thing and getting a compromised Congress to pass it is another, neither bill has been signed into law at this writing.

Until we get laws that put the students' needs ahead of those of the lenders or increased subsidies for the cost of a degree, parents of college-bound students need to adopt a strategy that minimizes their costs. Before we talk about ways to find money to finance college, it's worth it to spend a few moments to describe what happens to you if you can't repay a college loan.

Think of your worst nightmares; defaulting on one of these loans certainly qualifies as one. As I mentioned in the preceding chapter, the Education Department can now seize parts of borrowers' paychecks, tax refunds, and Social Security payments without a court order, a power that only the Internal Revenue Service, among federal agencies, regularly wields. What's more, there's no statute of limitations on collecting this debt as there is with most consumer debt.

In Collinge's book, *The Student Loan Scam*, he provides heartbreaking, horrific testimonials of borrowers who were hounded to pay their debt. He describes a man who borrowed about $7,500 in the 1980s who subsequently was found to have a form of autism that prevented him from finding a job. Despite being declared totally and permanently disabled by the Social Security Administration, he was still getting collection calls from the lender two decades later. Another borrower tried to repay her loan in full in order to save on interest costs, and the lender refused; instead, it garnisheed her wages so that it could collect the full amount. Still others took desperate measures, including leaving the country and committing suicide.

Your first plan of action should be to protect your college-bound kids from having their lives destroyed if they fall behind or are unable to make payments and wind up having their credit rating destroyed— even being deprived of a job in some circumstances. First, seriously consider whether you, the parent, ought to be the borrower and not your son or daughter—especially if you and/or your spouse has a well-paying and secure job. Unfortunately, a student loan is especially risky if my prediction about the retirement crisis is on target: if the first wave of Boomers is supposed to be able to retire in 2011 but can't afford to, my daughter's graduating class of 2011 is going to have a tough time landing jobs. Saddling an unemployed graduate with loan responsibility could very well mean sharing the same nightmarish fate as Collinge's.

On the other hand, if the parents' job situation is shaky or their income is below $60,000 or so and the son or daughter is an A student majoring in medicine or engineering or a similar lucrative pursuit that will enable him or her to repay the loan, the student loan may be the way to go. What's more, a few dozen wealthy colleges now offer "free rides" or "cheaper rides" to students from families with less than $60,000 in household income—and sometimes more (details at the end of this chapter)—so a loan may be unnecessary.

Until we get some genuine college cost reform in Washington, there are still steps you can take to lower college costs:

1. **Take advantage of free money.** Before we talk about cutting costs on borrowing for college, make sure that you take advantage of grants or scholarships.

Grants, scholarships: The bad news is that they are a small percentage of the total cost of college—and most kids won't get them because there's only so much money to go around. For example, in 2005 a mere 2.1% of students got tuition and fee waivers—which is essentially the same thing as a full scholarship. That same year need-based grants were awarded to more than 10% of undergraduate students but averaged only $3,300. That year merit-based grants were awarded to 7.9% of students, with an average award of $4,269, and federal Pell Grants were received by 26.8% of undergraduate students, with an average amount of $2,492—plus you probably won't even qualify for the latter unless your household income is less than $50,000. In summary, at best you're getting around $10,000 a year. But it's better than nothing and it's $10,000 less that you have to borrow and pay interest on for many years.

Most of Uncle Sam's money—about $7 billion—is distributed through **Pell Grants**. To get this money, you need to file the Free Application for Federal Student Aid (FAFSA), the federal government's instrument for finding out how much each family can pay for college. The FAFSA generates an expected family contribution that guides colleges in the distribution of federal funds and serves as a baseline for calculating eligibility. See the end of this chapter for the website that tells you how much of the bill you'll be footing.

Merit aid: This is when the college gives you a "reward" for having good SAT scores so that you'll apply and doing so will boost its rankings with *U.S. News & World Report*. Yeah, it doesn't make sense but every little bit of money helps, $4,000 or so worth in this case. **Keep in mind that SAT scores matter even more for merit aid than for admission; some schools even publish cutoff test scores for scholarships on their websites.** So if your kid's SAT scores are close to the cutoff, it's worth spending the money to take the test again and potentially save you $4,000 or so.

2. **Is your kid Harvard- or MIT-worthy but you're short on cash? Apply to a "rich" college that will subsidize most or all of the cost.** Most likely thanks to Sen. Chuck

Grassley's (R-IA) efforts to put a harsh glare on colleges with rich endowments who charge sticker-price tuition, more than 60 colleges have either replaced loans with grants or eliminated tuition altogether for those falling under certain income ceilings, most often under $60,000—some offer free education for everybody, regardless of income, under certain circumstances. See the end of this chapter for some sample colleges and the link on the internet to the complete list.

3. **Consider a state school, especially if you live in one of the 35 states that offer merit programs.** While the price tag for many state colleges has risen because of shrinking budgets due to economic doldrums, there are still a few bargains around. For example, Georgia's HOPE Scholarship allows any high-school student with a 3.0 GPA in core subjects to get free tuition at the state's public schools or up to $3,000 a year at its private ones—a fantastic deal. The reason Georgia can still afford to do this is that the revenues come from the state's lottery. Not all states are as generous as Georgia—the average grant is around $1,000—but it's worth checking out. The following website contains links to each of the state programs: http://www.nassgap.org/links.aspx.

4. **Consider one of the best bargains around: community colleges for the first two years, or maybe even all four!** The average annual community college tuition is $1,500 to $2,000, compared to $5,000 to $20,000 at four-year public schools and $30,000 to $50,000 at private four-year universities. What's more, some colleges have articulation agreements that make it easier for students to transfer from a community college to a four-year institution. Even better: some states, like California, Florida, and Pennsylvania, *guarantee* that students who receive an associate's degree will be admitted into one of the state's public four-year colleges. It gets even better: As of 2009, 17 states, including Nevada, Florida, Texas, and Washington,

have allowed community colleges to award bachelor's degrees, so you'll be saving big bucks for all four years of schooling, as long as your son or daughter doesn't mind commuting to college—as opposed to living there. Even if you live in a state that offers only a two-year program, community colleges are definitely a deal to consider. The only downside for students—depending on the personality of your son or daughter—is that it may be tougher to make friends at their new four-year college if they're transferring from another college. Many students may have already joined clubs or sororities and have made "ties that bind." **Make sure that the community college of your choice has an articulation agreement**.

Great resource for community colleges: http://www.ccweek. com. If you click on "Top 100," you will see how your local community college stacks up.

Resources for four-year community colleges: Unfortunately, I couldn't find a website with this information; presumably your child's high-school guidance counselor will keep up-to-date on whether your home state permits community colleges to offer four-year programs and which of those that do are within commuting distance.

5. **Most of us will have to borrow to afford paying for college—so keep your borrowing costs as low as possible.** Unfortunately, while a home-equity loan was a good option for my Dad, it may be a risky approach these days, given the melting housing market. So what options do you have? First, consider the federal direct lending program— and make sure your child does not apply to any college that Sallie Mae has convinced to drop the loan program, which means you're likely to be stuck with a high-cost "opportunity" loan. There are two components: a loan that parents take, and one for students. The **Parent Loan for Undergraduate Students (PLUS),** a federal loan

program for parents of college students, is the best deal around that Sallie Mae doesn't want you to know about; that's why less than 10% of the population has them. You can borrow up to the amount of college expenses, regardless of income. The **Stafford loan** is a federal loan taken by the student. While its interest rate is currently lower than on a PLUS loan, 6.8% versus 8.5% for the PLUS loan, there are limits on how much can be borrowed. (Don't ask me why the rate on the parent loan is higher since parents have better credit ratings.) That's why the best course of action is for your son or daughter to borrow up to the Stafford limits and you the parent take out a PLUS loan for the rest. Two websites with more info on the Stafford and PLUS loans are http://www.parentplusloan.com/ and http://www.staffordloan.com/.

6. **Whether you, your kids, or both of you wind up being the borrower, have a serious talk with your kids about choosing a major that will lead them to a career that will make the investment worthwhile.** Whenever one of my kids' friends tells me they are majoring in English, I have to bite my tongue—what kind of well-paying jobs can you land with an English degree? Some colleges actually charge more for majors that lead to low-paying jobs, such as education, fine arts, and journalism. (As a former journalist, I can attest that this is a poorly paying profession unless you're the next Katie Couric or Anderson Cooper.) In fact, if your child is seriously interested in careers in low-paying or hard-to-get professions such as these, he or she should definitely consider a state school/community college so that your/your child's debt load will be lower. Better yet, convince your kid to opt for a career that will enable him or her to pay back the loan. A good resource for hot job growth can be found on CNN Money's website: http://money.cnn.com/magazines/business2/nextjobboom/. Promising careers

range from physician's assistant to computer software engineer to college instructor (most likely because college professors often have tenure and pensions so that they can afford to retire).

7. **Needless to say, don't consult *U.S. News & World Report*'s rankings when considering a college.** A much better guide is *America's Best Value Colleges*, published by the Princeton Review.

8. **If your child has stellar grades and SAT scores, consider the universities that are now offering great deals—replacing loans with grants even if your household income is $200,000 or more in some cases.** This is one area where Congress has tried to do right and basically shame some of the richer private colleges into shaking their money trees. Here are some examples: Stanford University, which eliminates the parental contribution for families with annual incomes below $60,000; Yale University, ditto; Dartmouth College, which offers free tuition for students from families earning less than $75,000; Princeton University, which replaces loans with grants for all students who qualify for financial aid (you have to go online and apply to find out); Columbia University, which replaces loans with grants for families with incomes below $60,000; and Harvard University, which dramatically reduces the amount families with incomes below $180,000 have to spend. This is only a partial listing, because colleges are updating their criteria all the time. To find out current offerings, visit the following page on FastWeb.com: http://www.finaid.org/questions/noloansforlowincome.phtml.

Additional Web-Based Sources for Financial Help

Here are some additional sources:

Sources to help you get saving: www.wiredscholar.com, www.collegeboard.org, www.fastweb.com, www.scholarship-experts.com, www.kiplinger.com/tools/colleges.

Sources for financial aid: www.collegeboard.org, www.finaid.org.

Sources that explain the kinds of loans available: www.StudentLoanJustice.org, www.finaid.org.

PART IV

35 Million Americans Are Drowning in Credit Card Debt

Chapter 9

How Credit Card Debt, Home Equity Loans Get You Over Your Head in Debt

Credit card reform is one area where Congress has finally "done right" on behalf of its citizens. In May of 2009, President Obama signed into law a measure that bans interest rate hikes unless a consumer is more than 60 days late, requires credit card "promotional rates" to be in effect for at least six months, and requires the issuers to disclose the payoff time and total interest costs to consumers if they pay only the minimum balance on a bill. More importantly, it prevents card issuers from taking advantage of college kids by requiring any consumer under the age of 21 applying for a card to have a co-signer who is at least 21 years old unless the young person has the financial means to pay off the bill.

You have to hand it to the credit card industry—it is constantly thinking up new ways to profit at the expense of its customers, whether it's charging late fees, raising interest rates, or offering credit to people who don't even have jobs yet.

The practice of signing up college students for cards is particularly shameful. According to a survey released in 2008 by U.S. PIRG, 76% of students said credit cards had been marketed to them on or near college campuses, and nearly one-third had been offered a free gift to sign up. The result: many young people are in debtor's prison before they have their first full-time job. The average undergraduate owes $2,169 in credit card debt, with the average graduate student owing $8,612, according to Nellie Mae, a subsidiary of Sallie Mae.

In the same fashion that colleges profit off of Sallie Mae's "opportunity loans," they profited when students use credit cards. In 2008, *BusinessWeek* obtained more than two dozen confidential contracts between major schools and card-issuing banks; in some cases the colleges and alumni groups got larger payments from the banks if students use their school-branded cards more frequently. The credit card companies didn't even need to send solicitors to college campuses to contact the students because the colleges provided access to student e-mail addresses and phone numbers. So much for privacy laws.

How the Credit Card Industry Charges an Arm and a Leg in Interest

While the new law will probably have a significant impact on the spending habits of college students, it remains to be seen whether it will affect those of their parents' generation. Between the fees it collects and interest rates it charges, the credit card industry is hugely profitable. Sears, the third-largest MasterCard issuer in the world, earned 60% of its revenues from fees and interest rates charged on its cards in 2003, as opposed to the items sold in its stores. The obscene profits earned on credit cards is the reason why store clerks try to cajole you into taking out a store card with an "immediate savings of 10% off." Ironically, if you do apply for a bunch of store cards at once, it's very likely that your credit score will go down—you're seen as a risky spender—so card issuers will profit even more off the higher rates charged.

What's ironic is that at the same time Americans pride themselves on finding deals, sales, and bargains on merchandise—remember the slogan "I'm not gonna pay a lot for this muffler"?—card holders wind up paying many times the cost of these deals, sales, and bargains by only paying the minimum balance on a high-interest loan.

Thirty-Five Million Pay the Minimum Balance— and Therefore the Maximum in Interest

The 2004 PBS *Frontline* documentary, "The Secret History of the Credit Card," delivered a damning indictment of the $30 billion industry, which managed to get its card holders over their heads in debt without telling them. One of the most sinister practices is the bait-and-switch tactic of offering 0% introductory rates and lowering the monthly minimum payment requirement to entice consumers to borrow more. Currently, 35 million Americans make only the minimum payment each month.

Sadly enough, whether or not it's because our Neighbors to the North are more thrifty, or the government educates them to be that way, Canadians aren't drowning in debt. Credit card debt per Canadian household averaged $2,000 in 2006, compared to $8,000 in the U.S. Credit card debt is undoubtedly lower because some 73% of Canadians pay off their credit card balances every month, according to Kevin Stanton, president of MasterCard Canada. Unfortunately, I could not find any statistics on comparable percentage rates for Americans, which reflects poorly on our lack of concern with this issue.

In the same fashion that mortgage bankers used to have to abide by laws when it came to lending money, credit card issuers used to have to abide by usury laws that limited the interest rate they could charge. That all changed in 1980. Citibank, then based in New York, had lost $1 billion on its credit card business because the rate of inflation exceeded the interest rate New York's usury laws allowed it to charge.

The solution? Leave the state. Coincidentally, South Dakota's farm economy was also a mess, so the state needed all the revenues it could get. Then-Governor Bill Janklow readily agreed to convince the legislature to quickly pass a law that would enable Citibank to move its credit card operations to the state, bringing hundreds of high-paying jobs. Instead of losing $1 billion a year, Citibank generated nearly $30 billion in net revenue as of 2003. In 1981, Delaware passed similar legislation, which enticed Chase, Manufacturer's Hanover, and Chemical Bank to move there.

Bait and Switch with No Disclosure

The mortgage industry's Truth in Lending documents are so oblique that you'd need a lawyer to understand them, which explains why so many borrowers are saddled with dangerous loans. On the other hand, before the current law passed there was no comparable Truth in Carrying a Balance disclosure required of the credit card industry: disclosure was limited to the annual percentage rate, the fact that the rate may vary and by how much, the grace period for the repayment of the balance, the annual fee, etc. There were no requirements to show examples of the devastating effect of "compound interest in reverse"—that you will pay many times the price of an item at a point when you probably no longer own it.

Any attempt to protect the consumer was fought by the credit card industry, along with politicians who get campaign contributions from the industry and judges who uphold bad laws. When in 2001 California passed a law requiring credit card companies to disclose examples of the cost of credit with each bill, industry trade groups and credit card issuers sued to overturn it, and in May of that year a district judge did so, finding that a federal Office of Thrift Supervision regulation implementing the Home Owners' Loan Act prohibits state regulation of credit card notifications—preemption all over again.

On a Federal level, Sen. Dianne Feinstein (D-CA) introduced legislation similar to the California law in 2005 and in 2008, as did Sen. Daniel Akaka (D-HI) in 2007. A previous attempt by Akaka failed because Senate Banking Committee Chairman Richard Shelby, who receives millions of dollars in contributions from the credit card industry, objected that it would alter the Truth in Lending Act.

Treating Your Home Like an ATM

While consumer groups and decent politicians have finally forced banks to improve their credit card practices, to my knowledge there hasn't been a similar effort to stem the burgeoning increase in home equity loans—an even greater source of financial stress than credit card debt for many Americans. Before the 1980s, very few Americans took out home equity loans—the few exceptions were for emergencies and to bankroll their kids' college education. However, since the early 1980s, the value of home equity loans outstanding has ballooned more than 1,000-fold from $1 billion to more than $1 trillion, and nearly one-fourth of Americans with first mortgages have them.

For the most part, the increase in loans came as a result in a shift in marketing, largely led by Citigroup, which launched its "Live Richly" campaign in 2001, urging people to lighten up about money and helping persuade hundreds of thousands of Citi customers to take out loans. Several other major banks followed suit.

When the housing bubble started bursting in 2008 and the economy slowed, the portion of homeowners whose home equity lines were more than 30 days past due as of August 2008—that is, they were Living Poorly—was 55% above the average since the American Bankers Association began tracking the trend around 1990. So not only were the homeowners who were saddled with bait-and-switch ARMs in a pickle once housing prices started to slump, those who took out home equity loans were falling behind as well.

Then in early 2009 the American Bankers Association reported that delinquencies on home equity loans that are used to buy cars had reached record-high levels. Hold on now! Borrowing against an appreciating asset to buy a depreciating asset? Incredibly, this practice has become increasingly popular, especially in overpriced California, where reportedly one in three cars is purchased with home equity loans. The subsequent burst of the housing bubble that made it harder to get these loans is probably the explanation for the 43% drop in new-car sales in the Golden State in the first quarter of 2009. It's bad enough that the U.S. government bailed out General Motors, but it doesn't bode well that a big chunk of GM's and its competitors' revenues are dependent on rising home prices.

Home Equity in U.S. Is at Its Lowest Level Since 1945

An even more dangerous form of home equity loan is a cash-out refinancing, in which you suck all the equity out of your home to spend it or pay down debt, despite the fact you'll owe all that money back plus interest when you repay the loan—even if the home is worth less. Since 2005, cash-out refinancings have grown to one-third of all mortgage originations in the U.S.

The impact of this borrowing frenzy? The spiraling increase in the combination of cash-out refinancings, home equity loans, and home equity lines of credit has succeeded in reducing Americans' average equity rate to below 50% for the first time since 1945. What's more, while a 2003 survey by Economy.com (now Moody's Economy.com) indicated that 42% of borrowers were using the money for home improvements, 28% were using it to buy appliances and furniture. Unfortunately, even those who use the money to improve their home's value may regret it if they can't recoup the investment.

Not surprisingly, the banking industry that services our Neighbors to the North apparently hasn't defined "living richly" as living beyond your means by borrowing against your home. In an article entitled, "Canadians, Eager to Pay off Debt, May be Wary of Equity Loans," a survey of homeowners found that in the rare circumstances that home equity loans are used, it's to make home improvements.

As is the case with homeowners who are living in overpriced housing whose value may drop when they reach retirement age, the risk of home equity loans is that you're borrowing against your retirement future. With few exceptions, home equity loans should be used only for home improvements that will raise the home's ultimate selling price, and even in these circumstances they should be used cautiously, as I'll point out in the next chapter.

Solution to the Credit Card Debt/Home Equity Loan Dilemma: A Campaign for a Debt-Free America

Although we should be grateful that reform has reined in the credit card industry, we need to go a step further to educate Americans about the corrosive "cost" of paying compound interest in reverse— whether it's paying the minimum balance on a credit card bill, or taking out a home equity loan to buy a car. Fine-print disclosure isn't enough—we need a campaign to engage Americans to change their spending habits.

History offers a lesson. It wasn't the fine-print warning labels on cigarette packages that induced millions of smokers like me to kick the nicotine habit back in the early 1980s—it was then-Surgeon General C. Everett Koop's Campaign for a Smoke-Free America, whose goal was to get every American to kick the habit by the year 2000.

His effort convinced thousands of employers to launch educational campaigns at the workplace to entreat smokers to kick their habits, with impressive results. While in 1981, the year of Dr. Koop's confirmation, smoking took the lives of nearly 400,000 Americans—more than all deaths from alcohol, drug abuse, and car accidents combined—eight years later Koop's efforts reduced the number of smokers from 33% of the workforce to 26% of it. I'm one of the grateful beneficiaries of his campaign, having dumped a 15-year pack-a-day habit as a result.

What's exciting about living in the 21st century is that we don't need to depend on enacting laws to create reform when it comes to educating Americans; the internet has transformed communication—the ability to reach millions of people at the speed of light and at little or no cost. A similar effort to get Americans to kick their spending habits could have a much more transformative effect than simply enacting legislation that merely requires disclosure of the cost of certain kinds of debt, given the ability of the legal establishment to render the language so oblique that it's incomprehensible—as is currently the case with most fine print.

President Obama's Middle Class Task Force could launch a "Campaign for a Debt Free America by the Year 2017." Americans would resolve to pay down credit card balances and home equity loans, as well as paying off their mortgages earlier. In short, America's financial industry must stop profiting at the expense of its customers. I recommend that the Task Force coordinate its efforts with the Federal Trade Commission, whose motto is "Protecting American Consumers," and launch a national "Do You Know What Your Credit Card Debt Is Costing You?" awareness campaign, along with posting on its website the FDIC language I've included on the next page.

The website should also feature links to other websites where consumers can get more information about cutting down on debt, such as http://moneycentral.msn.com/articles/smartbuy/debt/contents.asp, http://moneycentral.msn.com/smartbuy/home.asp and http://www.myvesta.org/. In addition, the webpage would educate

Americans on how much money they can save by paying off their mortgage early, similar to the quiz "Test Your Mortgage Knowledge," as mentioned on page 74, offered on The Financial Consumer Agency of Canada's website that demonstrates the corrosive effect of "compound interest in reverse" and why it's better to have a shorter mortgage.

Until this effort gets launched, I'll offer details in the next chapter on how to get your finances in shape.

Making Only the Minimum Payment Maximizes Your Debt

Starting Balance	Interest Rate (APR)	Monthly Payments	Years to Pay Off	Total Interest Paid	Total Cost
$5,000	18%	The minimum ($100 the first month, gradually declines as balance does)	46	$13,926	$18,926
$5,000	18%	$100	8	$4,311	$9,311
$5,000	18%	$250	2	$986	$5,986

Note: The minimum payment is assumed to be 2% of the outstanding balance or $10, whichever is greater. Years are rounded to the nearest whole year.

Examples of Paying Double, Triple, and Quadruple the Cost of an Item over Time

Item	Price	Interest Rate	Years to Pay Off	Total Interest Paid	Total Cost
TV	$500	18%	8	$439	$939
Computer	$1,000	18%	19	$1,899	$2,899
Furniture	$2,500	18%	34	$6,281	$8,781

Note: All payments are the monthly minimum of 2% of the outstanding balance or $10, whichever is greater. Years are rounded to the nearest whole year.
Source: "Minimum Payments, Maximum Costs on Credit Cards," FDIC Consumer News—Summer 2003, September 15, 2003, www.fdic.gov/consumers/consumer/news/cnsum03/minmax.html)

Chapter 10

The Fix: How to Get Out of Credit Card Debtor's Prison

One of the few recently published books that addresses how Americans have been spending way too much for stuff is *Trading Up: The New American Luxury,* by Michael J. Silverstein and Neil Fiske. Unfortunately, besides the fact that its authors celebrate a trend that is self-destructive, the examples they offer are often downright laughable. Let me quote:

> "Perhaps the most startling traders-up we talked with were a group of consumers who were ecstatic about a product category that most people would like to forget—a washer-dryer combination...[that sold for] $2,000, compared to about $600 for a conventional washer-dryer combination. Believe it or not, consumers made the following comments about these European-style front-loading machines: 'I love them.' 'They are part of my family.' 'They are like our little mechanical buddies—they have personality.'"

The authors say that the consumers were "both men and women...who told us...[that the washer-dryer] makes them feel happy, like a better person, less stressed, prouder of their children, loved and appreciated, and accomplished."

Help me out here: Outside of a toilet, is there a more boring purchase? We are not talking about a car that transports you to a new destination or an iPod that allows you to listen to tunes, get directions, and check your mail—these are machines that basically do the same things my Mom's washer and dryer did 30 years ago, which is wash and dry your clothes. The only difference is that they cost 10 to 20 times as much.

What's ironic is that while price-cutting retailers Wal-Mart and Costco are seeing an uptick in sales in these recessionary times, once consumers enter these stores they may be paying bottom dollar for clothing and toys made in China—but they're likely paying top dollar for appliances that essentially haven't improved in decades. Part of the explanation for this spending spree is when it comes to certain machines, as illustrated in the washer-dryer example, consumers equate price with quality.

The second explanation for this spending spree is that most of us feel we can't live without items that didn't even exist 20 years ago, and we need to replace/upgrade these items as soon as a new version hits the market even if they don't offer features that make the investment worthwhile, from cell phones to PCs. We also way overpay for:

- Cars (gotta be SUVs—at least when the gas prices are affordable)
- Refrigerators (gotta be Sub-Zero, even if it doesn't contain a single feature that makes it worth the price)
- Sneakers (gotta be Nike)
- TVs (gotta be plasma)

And get this: the "pet accessories" industry has doubled in size in 10 years to revenues of $34-plus billion in 2004, *now larger than the toy industry.* It seems rather strange that an animal that used to live in the wild needs toys to stay happy—my dog's favorite "toy" is an animal bone, not a stuffed animal.

The Fix: Spend Less on Stuff, and Don't Replace Stuff That Doesn't Need Replacing

So, the alternative to paying too much for stuff we don't need is twofold:

1. Economize on products that you "consume" and/or stuff that decreases in value, such as vacations and TVs.

2. Hang onto stuff that has historically increased in value, whether it's your investments in stock mutual funds or the roof over your head.

It's a six-step process that involves refusing to buy things you don't need, spending less on what you do need, such as your car(s) and college education for your kids, and taking all the money you've saved and investing it for retirement. Specifically:

1. Spend less. Aim to pay off most credit cards and not carry a balance.

2. Consider buying a used car versus buying or leasing a new car.

3. Shop for a "competitively priced" college.

4. Get more money out of one of your biggest assets—your home—by owning it as long as possible and avoid taking out home equity loans.

5. Now that you've increased your savings, increase your contribution rate to your 401(k) account as soon as your employer allows you to do so.

6. Every time you get a windfall, whether it's a bonus or an inheritance, put that money in a Roth IRA or another tax-advantaged account.

Remember that the easiest route to retirement wealth is to stop: buying things you don't need, replacing stuff that's not worn out, paying too much for anything, and borrowing to buy anything if you can avoid it.

Step One: Cut the "Junk Spending" out of Your Household Diet

Thanks to aggressive marketing by credit card companies, the households who are in too much debt aren't just the ones who are considering bankruptcy, but also those who are being hounded by creditors and even those who are late with their bills every once in a while. It's the vast majority of Americans.

Here is a recent poll on MSN's Money website:

What best describes your situation?

- I have no debt: 15%
- I have some debt but I'm handling it: 40%
- I have enough debt to feel uncomfortable: 26%
- I dread opening the mail: 19%

First: Start Thinking About Stuff You Buy in a Whole New Way, by Asking Yourself Two Questions:

1. Do I really need this pair of shoes/cell phone/pair of jeans/plasma TV?
2. Will I be looking at these shoes/cell phone/jeans/TV next year and ask myself, "What was I thinking?"

Women: Do you wear ultrahigh heels with pointy toes because everybody else does, even if you have big ugly feet like mine? And how about capris—remember when those pants that end right below your knees were "in" a few years ago?

Guys: Do you think you need to trade your car in every three years so that yours looks snazzier than your neighbor's? Especially if it's a car that guzzles gas *and* your cash for upkeep and repairs?

Second: Don't Let Your Kids Boss You Around When it Comes to Money

We've witnessed a rarely documented role reversal when it comes to parents and kids—at least since I was one. When I was a kid, the only time you got presents was twice a year: at Christmas and on your birthday. These days not only can kids expect "presents" every time you take them to Wal-Mart and you pass the toy aisle to pick up cereal, but they're even telling their parents what grown-up purchases to buy. What's more, we are way overpaying for kids' stuff so that our kids' friends' parents will be impressed. Currently, middle-income parents spend more than $7,000 per child per year—and that's not counting college tuition! For example:

- Battery-powered sports cars are flying off the toy-store shelves at $500 a pop, not to mention high-end baby strollers retailing for $800-plus—a device that's no longer necessary when kids are walking on their own.

- Forty-three percent of 3- to 4-year olds have a TV set in their bedroom—I can hear those brain cells popping.

- Birthday parties can run up to $1,000 a pop.

- Kids are even telling parents what grown-up purchases to make, based on TV ads—more than $500 billion a year's worth of stuff. Word has it that the minivan was created because *kids* wanted a vehicle with more space. Then kids decided that minivans weren't cool—leading to the explosion in SUV sales.

Some tips:

- Kids should only get presents when it's a special occasion—Christmas or birthday—unless they're spending Christmas or birthday money, of course!

- Reconsider allowances. Depending on their age levels, kids should be told it's their duty to clean their rooms, do their laundry, and share in household chores such as doing the dishes.

- Save on the price of toys by buying them at garage sales—or at those "virtual garage sales" on eBay.

- Be creative in planning vacations that are frugal *and* fun. Rather than a week at a resort, how about vacations that teach, like nature spots that will wow your kids, such as the Grand Canyon, and museums that have free days or are free all of the time, e.g., Washington, D.C.'s National Air and Space Museum, the National Museums of American History and Natural History, and the National Zoo—and then throw in a day at a theme park at the end of the trip.

- Sure, you'll probably eventually splurge once on that Florida destination that features multiple mouse ears. But this needn't be more than a one-time indulgence—so at least your kids can tell their friends that they've "been there and done that."

Step Two: Realize What Unsecured Debt Can Cost You

Have you ever noticed how banks at least pretend to fall all over you to offer you a low interest rate on a fixed-rate mortgage—but until credit card reform went into effect, credit card companies typically didn't—or if it's a low rate, it's a teaser that will spike in a matter of months? The reason rates on car loans or mortgages are lower is because they are a secured debt, one in which the lender holds something that is at least as valuable as the amount of the loan, something known as collateral—essentially the lender "owns" your home or car until you pay it off. Think of collateral as a security deposit for the lender. On the other hand, a credit card purchase is considered a "risky debt" because the companies can't repossess that vacation you took or the outfit you no longer wear in the event that you fall behind on payments.

Credit card companies charge more for risky debt the same way insurance companies charge more for risky drivers. If you've ever been in a car accident that was determined to be your fault or if you have a teenage driver in your household, you've already experienced how car insurance companies charge higher premiums to risky drivers— or drivers who are perceived as risky. Since the companies can't recoup their losses, they have to charge you more in interest.

Step Three: Realize How Having Too Much Debt and Not Paying Bills on Time Can Cost You

As anyone who has ever watched *The Suze Orman Show* knows by now, everybody who uses a credit card has a FICO score (named after the company that invented it) that determines your creditworthiness. A credit score is the most influential measure not only of whether you'll get credit and how much you can borrow but also of how high your interest rate will be. Your credit score is determined by your history of paying bills on time, outstanding debt, length of credit history, and other factors. People who don't pay their bills on time pay more in interest because they "cost merchants more"—because the merchant has to spend money to send out dunning notices and pay collection agencies to go after that debt. What's more, people who have too much debt are considered risky debtors. When you improve your "rating," you'll improve your rate because you are a lower risk.

Here's what counts most on your credit report:

- History of paying on time: accounts for about 35% of your score.
- How much of your available credit has already been used: about 30%.

- Length of credit history: about 15%.

- Whether you have opened several credit accounts (i.e., those "store credit cards") in a short period: about 10%.

- Whether you have a "mix" of loans: credit card, auto, mortgage, and so on: about 10%.

You can get a free copy of your consumer disclosure every 12 months. Consumer disclosure is all the information in your credit file, as opposed to a credit report, which contains only some of it. The three credit report companies use one website, toll-free telephone number, and mailing address for consumers to order their report. You can get it by going online to www.annualcreditreport.com or calling 877-322-8228. Or you can print out the order form on the FTC's website: www.ftc.gov/credit and mail it to Annual Credit Report Request Service, P.O. Box 105281, Atlanta, GA 30348-5281.

Got credit problems? Avoid scams. Steer clear of credit repair agencies that charge a fee to improve your FICO score by removing negative information from reports. Some of the worst will try to convince you to declare bankruptcy, which may be the most self-defeating step you could take: A bankruptcy stays on your credit report for 10 years and can hinder your ability to get credit, a mortgage, or even a job. Your best approach is to try to negotiate with each lender.

Websites That Help You Cut Down on Debt

Find the best card at www.bankrate.com (click on "Credit Cards") or www.credit-card-applications-center.com.

Great places to get a "debt checkup": Try the site at http://moneycentral.msn.com/articles/smartbuy/debt/contents.asp. There are some terrific pointers, including a debt evaluation calculator and a savvy spending quiz to determine whether you're debt prone or debt free. The most amazing feature is a "spending analysis," in which you can actually drag in your bank account data (if you are a subscriber to an MSN email provider and your bank partners with MSN), and it will automatically analyze your bank account to see where your money is going: utilities, mortgage, and so forth! It's truly awesome. Also try http://moneycentral.msn.com/smartbuy/home.asp.

Step Four: Don't Treat Your Home Like an ATM

As I pointed out in the last chapter, it's bad enough that people are borrowing against their retirement nest egg by tapping home equity, but they are doing it to buy cars. A home equity loan should only be taken to make improvements on a home—and as I pointed out in Chapter 5, should only be done when you're ready to sell the house. If you've spent a fortune upgrading your kitchen 20 years before you're ready to sell, this high-priced improvement will be perceived as out-of-date by the next buyer.

A home equity loan may also be the most costly way to buy a car. What isn't disclosed to the prospective home-equity borrower is that while interest rates are probably lower on this kind of loan—and the interest may be deductible—the borrower very likely will stretch the payments over many years, therefore driving up actual interest payments, along with other undisclosed costs.

Whether you borrow against your home to buy a car or pay your kid's college tuition, the risk of these loans is that the value of your home may drop so you "owe" more than you own.

Step Five: Don't Let Your Wheels Take You for a Ride: Potential Savings of Buying Used Car Versus Leasing—More Than $15,000

Remember the book I quoted earlier, *Trading Up*, in which the authors rhapsodize about paying a bunch of money for stuff that is "emotionally important" to people? The problem with paying too much for a car is that you're buying a depreciating asset—something that loses its value as soon as you drive it off the lot. The second problem is that if you borrow, you'll be paying so much in interest that when it's time to trade it in you most likely will still owe money.

Here's how to avoid letting your wheels take you for a ride:

1. **Research the best buys in cars before you buy.** The last thing you want to do is pay a fortune for a car that you will spend a fortune repairing. The most trustworthy source of advice on how to spend wisely for just about everything is *Consumer Reports*. You'll find out how to get the most bang for your buck and avoid investing in a lemon. Details on how to sign up are found at the end of this chapter.

2. **Avoid long-term car loans, which can cause you to pay too much interest on a car that's overpriced to begin with.** Precisely because cars cost so much to maintain—at least the cars that aren't cars but gas-guzzling trucks—if you must borrow, keep the terms short. Since the sticker price of cars has shot through the roof because drivers equate expense with quality, long-term car loans have become very popular. In the recent past, cars were financed for three years at most, meaning that the loan was completely paid off when the car was fairly new. Now new-car loans are stretched as long as five or six years to keep the monthly payments low. While it doesn't feel as though you're paying a lot for your car when you consider low interest rates, four-figure rebates, low or zero down payments, and low monthly

payments, you are paying more for less, the same way paying the minimum balance on your credit card gets you over your head in debt. Before you know it, you are upside down—and we're not talking about an accident.

The downside of long-term loans: getting upside down, which means "head over heels" in debt. In financial lingo, upside down means that you owe more than your car is worth—possibly thousands more than what you could get for it in a trade-in because you've been able to postpone paying the principal. Unfortunately, the reaction of most car buyers is *not* to vow never to do this again but rather to continue the upside-down process to the next car; when trade-in time comes, they roll the dollars owed on the old car into the next long-term loan. A recent study showed that nearly 40% of new-car buyers were upside down on their trade-ins.

Because so many car owners are upside down, dealers are now peddling insurance called GAP insurance that promises to pay the difference between your vehicle's value and your loan balance if your car is totaled or stolen. Does it get any worse than this? You owe more than your car is worth *and* you're paying a premium for insurance to cover an unlikely event as well!

3. **Avoid leasing; it's essentially a long-term car rental, and you're paying through the nose for something you don't own.** Here are the downsides:

   a. You may be making a huge down payment and huge monthly payments on something you're not going to own.

   b. If you do decide to buy the car at the end of the lease, you'll end up paying thousands more than if you'd purchased it to begin with.

   c. You're bound to a lease agreement that imposes penalties if you default.

d. There may be mileage limitations—and you may pay a penalty if you exceed them. The leasing company wants to make sure you're not putting so many miles on the car that it can't be sold.

e. At the end of the lease, you may also be financially responsible to cover the costs of wear and tear.

The following chart shows the gigantic financial differences between leasing a car, borrowing money to buy a new car, and borrowing money to buy a used car.

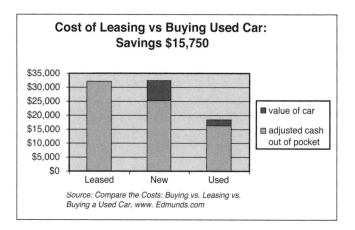

Bottom line: Because a car is a depreciating asset, it doesn't make sense to pay big bucks for the privilege of driving a car. Think about the difference between owning a stock and owning a car. When you sell your shares of Apple 20 years from now, they won't have lost value because you put too many miles or "scratches" on them. On the other hand, unless you own a vintage or discontinued Porsche, Jaguar, or other sought-after sports car, your car loses value, in fact starts losing it as soon as you drive it off of the lot.

4. To beat the high cost of wheels, pay cash for a "fairly new" used car. And, oh, yeah, forget the Porsche. The cheapest way to drive a car is to pay cash for a two- or three-year-old, well-maintained car that has a high ranking from *Consumer Reports* that is also cheap to insure, which rules out sports cars. Why? Insurance companies price "risk" the same way that lenders do—you'll pay a premium if there's a likelihood that the insurance companies will have to replace the car because somebody stole it. Sports cars can also be expensive to repair.

Sources to Help You Get Saving

Here are a couple of sources to help you save:

www.consumerreports.org: I can't stress enough that this is one of the best investments to make to help you "consume carefully." For $26 a year you get an excellent online source on how to get the best values on everything from dishwashers to digital cameras.

www.edmunds.com: This is a great place to help you compare car costs.

PART V

Real Campaign Reform That Puts Citizens, Not the Business Lobby, First

Chapter 11

How Big Business Owns Both Political Parties

In one of his regularly televised messages for constituents in 1963, Senate Republican Leader Everett Dirksen tried to explain to voters back in Illinois about a strange "creature" in the nation's capital—the Washington lobbyist.

"Now there has grown a particular sinister connotation about that word *lobbyist*," Dirksen intoned." You think of him as some sinister, skulking creature who is sneaking through the corridors of Congress...."

The scratchy black-and-white film of Dirksen's comments was shown at a National Press Foundation awards dinner in Washington in 2006. Laughter filled the room when Dirksen's granddaughter, Cissy Baker, played the film clip and noted that not much had changed in the past 43 years.

The usual depiction of the business lobby's corrupting influence is overbidding for government contracts. But as we've seen, the most pernicious activity is fighting laws that protect citizens and enacting bad laws that help the financial industry at the expense of its customers.

Never watch politics or sausage being made, as the saying goes. But if the electorate knew about the backroom deals that are conducted on Capitol Hill and how big business throws money at Congress, they might get hopping mad and throw the bums out. Former Congressman Joe Scarborough, a Republican from Florida, described the unsubtle way that peanut farmers threw cash at him to buy his vote.

"My first term in Congress I was proud to vote for a plan to abolish all farm subsidies within seven years," Scarborough recounts in his book *Rome Wasn't Burnt in a Day*. "The Freedom to Farm Act...had been made toothless by a series of farm-subsidy bills. In 1997, it was time to reauthorize a slew of farm bills, so I began getting calls from lobbyists."

Lobbyists representing peanut interests began streaming into his office as the peanut subsidy vote approached. "'Thanks for coming guys,' I said to the group crammed into my office, 'but as you probably know, I promised to vote against your program when I was running for office.'"

A few days later Scarborough's chief of staff walked into his office and tossed an envelope on his desk. "The package contained thousands of dollars in checks from the peanut industry along with a note thanking me for taking the time to visit with them."

When Scarborough expressed outrage to his chief of staff and demanded that he return the checks to the donors, the staffer "smiled his all-knowing smile, closed the door behind him and kept the money from the peanut lobbyists safe and secure in the Joe Scarborough for Congress Re-election Campaign."

Unfortunately, many politicians who are honorable enough to try to do the taxpayers' bidding and abolish wasteful programs get frustrated with their compromised colleagues and wind up quitting. The result is that we taxpayers are stuck with a majority of elected officials who not only take legal "bribes" from big business but also have the gall to thank the honest politicians who dare to support good legislation for causing the greedy ones to receive more bribes.

When former Congressman Dan Miller (R-FL) attempted to kill subsidies to sugar growers in 1996, members of Congress who voted against him privately thanked him for introducing the bill because it brought them extra contributions from the sugar PACs, or Political Action Committees, organizations that raise money for candidates.

Each year, Former Rep. Tim Roemer (D-IN) tried to get his colleagues to vote for a measure that would eliminate the space station from the federal budget—"because...it's about a hundred billion dollars over what it's supposed to be"—to no avail. After the vote: "I've had a host of members come up to me and say, 'You make the right argument....If this was a secret ballot we would certainly be with you in overwhelming numbers.'" (Presumably the lobby pressuring the members was government contractors who benefit from the space station's budget, not NASA itself.)

Roemer also had the temerity to try to tackle one of the sleaziest industries of all, gambling, in which "the house usually wins"—otherwise, how would the industry make any money? "I introduced an anti-gambling bill which would restrict gambling on college games. And that bill I think has been successfully bottled up by both the Republican and the Democratic leadership in the Judiciary Committee."

When most Americans think of the phrase "corrupt Congress," they think of Jack Abramoff or Bridges to Nowhere earmarks. But as we've seen, one of the most sinister forms of corruption is businesses that "bribe" politicians to allow them to profit at the expense of the electorate, whether it's subsidizing rich farmers or enabling banks to sell bait-and-switch ARMs, or allowing Sallie Mae to dominate the lending industry with expensive student loans.

How Congress Creates Jobs for Life—Either in Congress or Lobbying Congress

Congress has developed an elaborate system to maintain the status quo. It renders enforcement agencies toothless and ensures that congresspeople will have jobs as lobbyists if they don't get reelected, at the same time using a form of PAC that allows incumbents to donate to each other so that they can outspend any newcomer who would dare run against them.

Guess what happens when politicians have to talk about campaign contributions—never mind what happens when they actually end up voting on issues affecting these contributions. In a hearing before the Senate Governmental Affairs committee in 2006, the topic was so-called leadership PACs, which collect contributions and dispense the money to congressional allies with the expectation that they'll return the favor when it comes to voting on key legislation. The contribution limits aren't as strict on leadership PACs as with other campaigns because they don't spend the money on election campaigns—they give it to each other. It's basically "incumbent protection."

Why do we care about bad money? It's not just being bribed to vote the wrong way on legislation, it's free money to fund your campaign when the election rolls around so that you're assured of lifetime employment in Congress. The most onerous role the money plays is to keep inept and corrupt incumbents in their jobs because it frightens challengers who don't have the same deep pockets out of the race—a main reason why 98% of incumbent House members won reelection in 2004 and good guys like Scarborough, Miller, and Roemer end up dropping out.

During the hearing, the senators seemed virtually unanimous in their view that when it comes to influence peddling, "the status quo stinks," as Sen. Joseph I. Lieberman (D-CT), the recipient of more than $3 million from lobbyists and lawyers from 2003 to 2009, put it. The senators sounded as though they were at an Alcoholics Anonymous meeting, powerless to overcome their reliance on lobbyist cash. "It's out of control," lamented Sen. George V. Voinovich (R-OH), a recipient of $573,000 from lobbyists and lawyers over a five-year period, according to the Center for Responsive Politics. "And it's about time we collectively think about how we can get off the treadmill."

Somehow it's hard to take them seriously, given that Sen. Rick Santorum (R-PA), the man designated by Senate GOP leadership to draft a reform bill, ranked fifth of the 535 members of Congress in receipts from lobbyists and lawyers: $519,000 in 2005 alone.

Not surprisingly, the proposals getting the most serious consideration during the hearing were relatively minor: whether to ban lobbyist-paid lunches or a few million dollars' worth of privately funded trips. It doesn't take a rocket scientist to figure out why: by making only minor changes, they can pay lip service to reform instead of actually carrying it out.

What's more, guess how many of the chest-thumping 16 members of the committee sat through the entire hearing? Two. Maybe we need to broadcast these hearings on YouTube.

And if you think a Democratic majority will mean less "incumbent protection," think again: 10 of the top 20 recipients of Leadership PAC money in 2008 were Democrats.

The second-most-blatant piece of evidence that Congress has no interest in ending corrupt campaign practices is the attempt to fire the cops on the beat who have oversight over their activities. It's only because Scott Thomas, the chairman of the Federal Election Commission until January 2006, was doing a good job that he was all but out the door several times. Only the intervention of like-minded members of Congress led by Sen. John McCain (R-AZ) and Sen. Russ Feingold (D-WI) prevented him from being replaced.

In addition, in the same fashion that the fines levied on student lenders by state attorneys general amount to mere slaps on the wrists—essentially the "cost of doing business"—the FEC's attempt to increase its audits and fines are shrugged off by members of Congress, said Kent Cooper, co-founder of PoliticalMoneyLine.

Bipartisan Revolving Door

At the same time Leadership PACs often guarantee a lifetime job in Congress—even in 2008 when the Democrats were the majority, there were only 33 open seats, the lowest in decades—coziness with the lobbying industry ensures that a lobbying job will be almost certain in the rare event of a defeat.

The situation was exacerbated in 1995, when then-House Republican Whip Tom DeLay of Texas and conservative activist Grover Norquist launched what they called their "K Street Project." The idea: Republicans would take over the big lobbying firms as successfully as they already had taken hold of the House of Representatives.

They went after not only campaign contributions for GOP candidates, but also high-paying jobs for members of Congress who wanted to enter the private sector. Their message was clear: if you want to get along with us, get yourself some Republicans.

There are now 15,000 lobbyists in Washington, 27 for every member of Congress. According to the Center for Responsive Politics, lobbying outlays have more than doubled from $1.44 billion in 1998 to $3.28 billion a decade later—so much for McCain-Feingold.

According to Public Citizen, between 1998 and 2004 some 42% of former House members and 50% of former senators who were available to do so became registered lobbyists. While members of Congress technically have a one- or two-year "cooling-off period" before becoming a lobbyist, the requirement is toothless because it's very likely that the former members will take a "temp job" with a lobbying firm as a "strategic adviser" or some similar title during the so-called cooling-off period, helping to sign up clients.

Why do we care about the revolving-door trend? Because congresspeople who have their eye on a K Street job tend to draft legislation that benefits their future employers, says political science professor Adolfo Santos in his book *Do Members of Congress Reward Their Future Employers?* Studying the behavior of the 659 House members who served at least two terms between 1976 and 2000, Santos found that not only do these politicians submit more business-friendly bills during their last session, but they are more likely to get them enacted into law.

Bipartisan K Street Influence

Nobody should be surprised that, despite a Democratic majority in Congress, nothing will change when it comes to K Street's influence—it simply means that lobbyists are now writing more checks to Democrats.

For example, when President Obama arrived at the Mandarin Oriental Hotel for a fund-raising reception on June 18, 2009, the new White House rules were in order: no lobbyists allowed. But at the same hotel the next day, registered lobbyists had not only been invited to attend an issues conference with Democratic leaders, they had also been asked to come with a $5,000 check if they wanted to stay in good favor with the party's House and Senate reelection committees.

According to *The New York Times*, in mid-June Democrats sent an urgent appeal to lobbyists on behalf of the Democratic Senatorial Campaign Committee and the Democratic Congressional Campaign Committee. "Please note that the Friday Issues Conference is NOT subject to lobbyist restrictions, though the event is intended for personal contributions only," an official from the Democratic Senatorial Campaign Committee told lobbyists in an email message. "The Issues Conference is separate from the...events with President Obama."

In addition, 'corporate welfare'—either in the form of tax breaks for profitable companies or subsidies for prosperous farmers that don't need them—will amount to $100-plus billion in direct outlays under a Democratic Congress, compared to the last GOP Congress, which featured some $92 billion a year in subsidies," according to the Cato Institute. Former Congressman Joe Scarborough probably isn't surprised to learn that the Democrats are as generous to rich farmers as his former Republican colleagues: the Democratically controlled House passed a five-year farm bill with a cost of $286 billion, with two-thirds of these subsidies directed to the richest 10% of farmers, according to USDA calculations.

Probably the most insidious role that corporate lobbying plays is tax avoidance—one of the least-talked-about causes of our ballooning federal budget deficits. As Service Employees International Union (SEIU) President Andy Stern points out, while the tax rate on corporate income for the largest corporations is set at 35%, most companies pay much less: these revenues as a share of the federal budget have shrunk from 28% in the 1950s to a mere 2% today. It's amazing that more than half of the Fortune 500 could make a case that they needed a 21% cut in taxes from 2001 to 2003, given that their pretax profits rose by 26% during that period.

Congress Has a Higher Standard of Living Than the Taxpayers Who Subsidze It

What's outrageous about politicians on the take is that "the bribe" is heaped on top of perfectly adequate compensation that is bankrolled by taxpayers. The current salary for rank-and-file members of the House and Senate is $174,000 a year, more than four times the U.S. median wage. Members of Congress can also expect to receive a cost-of-living adjustment annually unless they vote not to—at the same time that the median wage in America rose by only 1% a year on average between 2002 and 2005, two percentage points less than inflation.

Unlike most of their constituents, members of Congress are also eligible for a pension if they've completed 20 years of service, based on the average of the highest three years of a salary—essentially the same perk as a defined benefit pension in the private sector for long-term employees for those rare employees who are lucky enough to still have one. As of 2006, 290 members of Congress were receiving an average pension of nearly $61,000 a year, compared to a typical pension of around $19,000 for the rare private-sector employee lucky enough to have one.

Given the average age of these elected officials, it's not surprising that a huge number of them will collect a pension. Sen. Robert Byrd (D-WV), the longest-serving senator in U.S. history, will be 95 at the end of his ninth term; Sen. Daniel Akaka (D-Hawaii) will be 88 at the end of his third term, if he's reelected. So it's no surprise that the average age of a senator is 60—the oldest ever—and the average age of a congressperson is 55—the oldest in more than a century.

That $61,000-a-year retirement paycheck is pretty hefty, considering that these folks don't even put in a five-day workweek. Despite the fact that House Speaker Nancy Pelosi vowed to institute the radical concept when the Democrats took over the House in 2007, in the entire year, Congress worked only three five-day workweeks, according to

Dick Morris and Eileen McGann in their book *Fleeced*. What's more, even when members of Congress do show up, their work days are too often focused on commending a football team for winning a bowl game or naming a post office after a judge rather than enacting legislation that benefits the folks who pay their salaries.

Someone needs to remind members of Congress that there's a reason their approval rating of 14% in 2009 was lower than that of former President George W. Bush compared to Obama's ratings of 62% in some polls. In fact, the 75% of the population who disapproved of Congress in 2008 is just shy of the record high of 78% in 1992.

When you think about it, although President Bush botched the Hurricane Katrina rescues and launched an ultimately unpopular war in Iraq, at least he tried to accomplish things, such as improving education with the No Child Left Behind Act, helping Iraq develop a democracy, creating Homeland Security, and developing better border control. Except for Senators McCain and Kennedy and Rep. George Miller, along with the six reform-minded Senators mentioned in Chapter 4, I can think of few, if any, legislators with decades of service in Congress who attempt to accomplish anything that significant— and, as we've seen, the ones who do often leave office out of frustration. When someone mentions the words "famous congressman," the stories are usually of members involved in scandal, like Sen. Bill Jefferson of Louisiana, who was indicted for pressing businessmen for kickbacks in exchange for setting up ventures in several African nations (he has pleaded innocent) in 2007, or Rep. Randy Cunningham of California, who in 2005 pleaded guilty to taking bribes from military contractors.

While most people who are elected President will lose sleep over how history records their legacy, it appears that too many in Congress are perfectly happy to just show up at work and do the bidding of the business lobby because it's rare that someone will publish a report card on their productivity or lack thereof.

Chapter 12

The Fix: Replacing Corrupt Politicians with Ones Who Work for Taxpayers

Pretend Campaign Reform That Doesn't Get at the Root of the Problem

We've seen how the lack of a citizens' lobby allowed the demise of defined benefit pensions, and their replacement by the "pretend pension," the 401(k) plan, which too frequently features "play money" stock matching contributions. The deregulation of the mortgage industry coupled with the prevailing Too-Big-to-Fail bailout mentality on Capitol Hill resulted in the rescue of bad banks—not to mention the compensation of their reckless leaders—but little help for homeowners, who are apparently considered Small Enough to Fail. At the same time, Sallie Mae's lobby made college loans expensive for students and impossible to escape in bankruptcy. And until 2009 legislation was passed, the credit card industry got away with ripping off customers with double-digit interest rates without disclosing the cost of the debt.

Why do we care about campaign reform? Because none of the remedies to Americans' financial woes offered in this book will come about unless the business lobby is put out of business—regardless of whether we've got a Democratic or Republican majority in Congress.

For example, a bill that would require lawmakers to identify lobbyists who assemble multiple donations and turn them over to the candidates went into effect in March of 2009. Among other things, the law sharply curtails the ability of lobbyists to trade gifts and travel for access to Congress, ends the practice of discounted flights on corporate jets, and tightens the "cooling-off period" before they can become lobbyists.

However, that's not the problem with Congress. The biggest problem is not gifts, trips, attack ads, and cooling-off periods. And simply identifying bundlers doesn't get at the real issue. That's because the typical bundler does **not** reimburse the donors, as was the case with Norman Hsu, the textile-importer-turned-fugitive who cobbled together $800,000 from voters for then-Sen. Hillary Clinton's Presidential campaign. The more typical "bundler" is the CEO of a company who either implicitly or explicitly threatens his or her top brass reports with the loss of a bonus if they don't contribute—even the loss of the job itself. The CEO then "bundles" the contributions and hands it to the candidate in question.

If you have any doubts as to whether Democrats are equally compromised when it comes to campaign contributions, consider the case of Sen. Christopher J. Dodd of Connecticut. As Democrats prepared to take control of Congress after the 2006 elections, a top boss at the insurance giant American International Group, Inc. told colleagues that Dodd was seeking reelection donations and he implored company executives and their spouses to give.

The message in the Nov. 17, 2006, e-mail from Joseph Cassano, AIG Financial Products (AIG-FP) chief executive, to the division's top brass was unmistakable: Dodd was "next in line" to be chairman of the Senate Banking, Housing and Urban Affairs Committee, which oversees the insurance industry, and he would "have the opportunity to set the committee's agenda on issues critical to the financial services industry. Given his seniority in the Senate, he will also play a key role in the Democratic Majority's leadership," Cassano wrote in the message, obtained by *The Washington Times*.

Dodd's campaign quickly hit pay dirt, collecting more than $160,000 in just a few weeks from employees and their spouses at

AIG-FP in Wilton, Connecticut, in the days before he took over as the committee chairman in January 2007. Months later, the senator transferred the donations to jump-start his failed 2008 presidential bid. Dodd's alleged "payback" to AIG became evident in early 2009 when he emerged as a central figure in the government's decision to let executives at the failing AIG collect more than $218 million in bonuses, according to the Connecticut attorney general—even as the company was receiving billions of dollars in assistance from the Troubled Asset Relief Program (TARP). (A spokesman for Dodd told *The Washington Times* that any contributions from executives who got a bonus would be donated to charity.) Dodd acknowledged that he slipped a provision into legislation in February that authorized the bonuses, but insisted the Treasury Department asked him to do it.

Dodd's move generated national outrage and put the Obama administration in the position of trying to collect the bonuses after they were distributed. It also may have endangered Dodd's reelection chances in 2010 as his popularity tumbled in his home state.

The Federal Election Commission's Decision to Allow Employers to Coerce Their Employees to Lobby

The practice of allowing a company's top brass to pressure employees to contribute and then bundle contributions came about not as a result of legislation openly debated by Congress but as a result of a little-known "advisory opinion" by the Federal Election Commission. In its 1975 "SUN-PAC" opinion, the FEC permitted corporations to solicit Political Action Committee (PAC) contributions not just from their stockholders but also from their managerial employees. According to the ruling, businesses can be most "explicitly political" with members of their "restricted" class, defined as most managerial employees and shareholders. When talking to these people, the top brass can officially endorse candidates and "encourage" an employee to either donate to or work for a candidate. On the other hand, when talking politics with rank-and-file workers, allegedly the most that companies may undertake is "offering guides that list the views of all candidates."

An Executive Fights Back

While we don't know whether any executives at AIG refused to heed Cassano's plea, one former Bank of America executive got so fed up with being coerced into contributing that he took action against his former employer. Duncan Goldie-Morrison alleged in an arbitration filing before the National Association of Securities Dealers in November of 2003 that he and others were ordered to make political contributions. "Because he refused to look the other way and play along with what I would call corporate shenanigans, he was terminated," said his lawyer, Sean O'Shea.

If Bank of America were to contend that the action was taken as a result of bitterness from, say, being passed over for a promotion, it would be a tough argument to sell. Goldie-Morrison was one of the highest-ranking executives at the bank's corporate and investment-banking division, building it into one of its biggest revenue contributors, accounting for about 18% of the bank's total earnings.

Goldie-Morrison isn't alone. When surveyed anonymously, a significant number of the top brass report feeling pressured to contribute. *CFO Magazine*'s 2004 survey of chief financial officers found that 24% of respondents said that not giving to their corporate PAC could be detrimental to their careers. One former Morgan Stanley employee interviewed for a 2004 article in *Investment Dealers' Digest* said memos would be sent asking employees to donate to the company's PAC and employees who didn't were sent a follow-up memo—a sign that managers were keeping track of who was naughty and who was nice.

"I distinctly remember feeling pressured to donate to...PACs that were aligned with the firm's interest," said the former employee. "You definitely felt like it was in your best interest to donate, even if you didn't believe in it."

How Poorly Paid Middle Management and Rank-and-File "Involuntary 401(k) Shareholders" Are Pressured to Lobby

But an even more nefarious effort than getting the top brass to cough up money is the role of business PACs in intimidating their lower-paid reports into essentially lobbying for their interests—creating a fake grass-roots effort.

Greg Casey is president of the Business Industry Political Action Committee, or BIPAC, a coalition of business owners and business associations who convince employees to lobby for legislation that favors employers at the expense of the employee. According to Casey, BIPAC was started in 1963 because business leaders observed—incredibly—that business was not getting enough bang from its campaign bucks compared to the unions. While 19% of voters who cast a ballot in biennial elections belonged to a union household in the early to mid-1990s, by 2000 it had risen to 27%. However, despite the recent raft of corporate scandals, says Casey, polling shows that most workers continue to trust their own employer. (Or more likely they're inclined to do what their employer tells them because there will be repercussions if they don't.)

As a result, the "virtual lobbying effort" known as the Prosperity Project, or P2 as BIPAC calls it, was started in 2000; by 2004, more than 900 companies had Prosperity Project websites, reaching about 20 million workers, according to Casey. It's a very cost-effective approach—rather than having to pay for plane tickets to jet employees into Capitol Hill, the employees can be "encouraged" to send e-mails to their congresspeople—they don't even have to compose the e-mails; they're already prewritten.

Under the program, employees receive company e-mails and paycheck stuffers driving them to their employer's public-affairs website. When employees go to the website, they can click on "Top Issues" to learn the company's position on the issues. If they click on "About Your Elected Officials" and enter their zip code, up come the voting records of their House and Senate representatives on key issues, complete with green check marks and ugly red Xs. If the Xs make you mad, you're urged to click on "Take Action," which lets you e-mail your local senators or House members. The letters are already written or you can write your own.

Casey told a *National Journal* reporter, "We want [employers] to tell employees how to register, how to take out an absentee ballot, and tell them how a representative's views influence, for example, a worker's 401(k)." Presumably, Casey means that if an honorable congressman like George Miller had drafted legislation requiring employers to match employee 401(k) contributions in cash, rather than risky—and potentially worthless—company stock, the employees would be encouraged to e-mail Miller's office, or more likely, their Congressperson, to attack the legislation. Most likely the "spin" would be that outlawing a stock match would force the company to sell its shares, causing the share price to drop and threatening employee job security. Given that the National Association of Manufacturers (NAM) is currently a member of the Coalition on Employee Retirement Benefits, which lobbies Congress to reduce retirement benefits by fighting for the "right" to match 401(k) contributions in company stock instead of cash, it wouldn't be surprising.

While Casey insists that employees are not pressured to lobby—"We do not lobby on issues and do not intend in any way to convince employers to lobby"—it seems clear that companies have no business even "suggesting" that employees get involved in influencing legislation or campaigning for candidates. If I'm working for a company that makes gas-guzzling cars that pollute the atmosphere, that doesn't mean I favor gas guzzlers and want Congress to lower emissions standards; it might just be the only job I could get at the time. What's more, I may have joined the company with the hope of convincing management that the better approach to growing market share would be to make fuel-efficient cars rather than maintaining the gas-guzzling status quo.

The Fake Grass-Roots Effort Opposing Unionization

While I can't offer concrete evidence, there's a good chance that this "fake grass-roots effort" is the reason that, in early 2009, many members of Congress were rethinking their support of the Employee Free Choice Act (EFCA), which would let workers opt for unionization simply by signing cards rather than through secret ballot elections, which give employers the ability to campaign against unionization and essentially intimidates employees into voting against it. The fact is that most Americans support unionization—regardless of the "color of their collar"—most likely because most "salaried" (nonunion) employees also benefit when the "hourly" workers succeed in getting benefits such as healthcare and pension coverage, along with wage increases. In a January 2009 poll by Hart Research Associates, 78% of Americans favored legislation that would make it easier for workers to bargain with their employers and 73% favored the Employee Free Choice Act.

Unfortunately, since the business lobby's voice is what currently counts in Washington, even key Senate Democrats, along with one would-be Democrat, were wavering in their support of EFCA in early 2009. For example, Arkansas Senator Blanche Lincoln apparently was convinced that unionization destroys jobs, saying, "I have 90,000 Arkansans who need a job; that's my No. 1 priority," calling the legislation "divisive." (Apparently, Lincoln's other pressure was the next election since she was running for office in a state that President Obama lost, 59% to 39%.) Sen. Arlen Specter, a Pennsylvania Republican who subsequently switched parties, who was initially more supportive of the bill, admitted that his change of heart came about because: "I'm being lobbied on it very, very heavily."

It is not unreasonable to suspect that Specter and his colleagues' change of heart was a result of the "virtual" lobbying effort by the employees of member companies of NAM, along with employees of other antiunion companies, such as Wal-Mart. When I went to the page on Prosperity Project's website displaying sample campaigns of their corporate partners, I got a peek at how employees of NAM's member companies are expected to lobby for their employers. On the webpage titled "Take Action with NAM's Contact Congress," employees are encouraged to send "draft messages" to their lawmakers on the following topics: "Tell Members of Congress to Oppose the 'Employee FORCED Choice Act,' in Any Form" and "Tell Your Senators to Oppose the Paycheck Fairness Act." So these employees are essentially called upon to ask their elected representatives to vote against legislation that would enable them to join a union and make it more difficult for them to sue for wage discrimination.

Pressuring the Rank and File

Reality shows that the rules against pressuring the rank and file are frequently broken and rarely is there a consequence, especially since the judges often side with the employers. One example of rank-and-file coercion is Enron: not only did the employees lose their jobs when the company tanked *and* lose their 401(k) savings, which were 100% invested in Enron stock, but employees had complained that management coerced them into contributing to the corporate PAC.

In fact, seven years after SUN-PAC went into effect, the International Association of Machinists and Aerospace Workers went to court, claiming that the FEC was allowing companies like General Motors Corporation to pressure its rank-and-file employees into giving money to corporate PACs. The union claimed the solicitations were "inherently coercive" because immediate supervisors were approaching employees. Unfortunately, the U.S. Court of Appeals for the District of Columbia Circuit sided with the FEC.

Even if there were rules against the top brass bullying the rank and file, the term "management" can be defined as a low-paid restaurant manager. For example, Andrew Fitzgerald, a cook at an Outback Steakhouse restaurant who got promoted in 1995 to kitchen manager, a position with a $22,000 base salary, was asked to sign a consent form authorizing Outback to regularly deduct $5 from each paycheck. "Let's face it," said Fitzgerald, "when the big boss asks you to do something—and not doing that may hinder reaching your ultimate goal—you're going to do it." Five bucks may not sound like a lot, but if you have hundreds of restaurants it adds up—in fact, Outback's PAC was the largest of its kind in the restaurant industry.

Most of Fitzgerald's peers were only vaguely aware of the PAC's goals, which included opposing an increase in the minimum wage, fighting the creation of a national healthcare plan, and supporting a California bill that would have required unions to obtain annual written permission from their members before they could use their dues for political activity—rather ironic, given that employers aren't obligated to seek written permission to use employee "donations" to this effect. Given that the managers' measly $10-an-hour salary was less than twice today's minimum wage, it's hard to believe that they'd be sympathetic with a union-bashing initiative, much less fighting an increase in the minimum wage or better healthcare coverage.

Along with pressuring low-paid managers to lobby, permitting companies to pressure their rank-and-file workers because they are shareholders—despite the fact that ownership of the shares isn't voluntary but "accidental" because the employer is unwilling to match their 401(k) contributions in cash—creates a phony grass-roots effort that most likely many members of Congress don't realize is phony, or at least coerced. It seems amazing that there hasn't been a groundswell of resistance to this kind of pressure—perhaps it's a function of these tough economic times that most Americans have resigned themselves to keeping their mouths shut in order to keep their jobs.

We Need to Abolish Business PACs and Replace Them with Citizens' PACs

Unfortunately, the Constitution prohibits us from outlawing the business lobby or prohibiting employers from pressuring the rank and file to lobby, because lobbying is considered "the right to petition the Government for redress of grievances"—our forefathers must be rolling over in their collective graves at this interpretation. That leaves us no choice but to empower a genuine citizens' lobby that represents taxpayers. Currently, any campaign reform discussions "stay inside the Beltway" and good reform gets killed by greedy and needy politicians and replaced by "fake reform."

We need a national citizens' PAC that not only issues "report cards" on Congresspeople that are publicized in the media in their districts, but also encourages honest candidates to run for office and replace them. We are now witnessing an era in America in which many of its citizens have never been poorer, with 80% of them unable to retire, half unable to afford what now amount to overpriced homes—and therefore losing out on a vital retirement asset—and millions paying through the nose for higher education and healthcare. We need a new American revolution against the business lobby and those in Washington who enable it and do its bidding.

The good news is that a citizens' PAC has emerged that is serious about campaign reform. Rather than simply trying to convince the incumbent members of Congress to mend their evil ways, the Accountability Now coalition is actively seeking to replace members of Congress. Its members include the Service Employees International Union (SEIU), MoveOn.org, and Democracy for America.

In the same fashion the Obama campaign took advantage of the internet to raise millions of dollars in small donations, Accountability Now's creators, bloggers Glenn Greenwald of salon.com and Jane Hamsher of firedoglake.com, raised $500,000 between March of 2008 and March of 2009 alone. Soliciting donations from their supporters, the bloggers say they are planning to recruit candidates to challenge out-of-touch Democrats in Congress.

"We need to get people in office who are closer to Main Street than K Street, that are closer to the grass roots," says Accountability Now's executive director Jack Hauser, who also agrees that corporate PACs play a deceptive role in politics. Beltway insiders say that unfortunately even honorable members of Congress are vulnerable to potentially phony corporate PAC campaigns because they are stressed and understaffed. Along with depending on an overworked staff of seven or eight people and a budget of barely $1 million, they may have multiple issues to follow. In addition to constituent services they may have to stay on top of foreign policy, ERISA, and committee assignments—a challenging array of issues. For that reason, "corporate PACs can trick members into thinking that there is a grass-roots effort," Hauser says.

Hauser agrees that the current campaign reform strategy of simply trying to convince current members of Congress to vote for it needs to be dumped for one that raises money to support candidates who will replace incumbents who aren't answerable to their constituents in the primaries.

"We think that contributions to oppose members who have fallen out of touch with their district can get great 'bang for their buck' because the message will really resonate with voters," Hauser says. "We want to change the incentives for members of Congress—we want them to change on their own and become more responsive."

Another admirable group in Washington is the Center for Responsive Politics, which for more than 25 years has tracked money in U.S. politics and its effect on elections and public policy, and is the source for most of the material on "money and politics" in this book. In short, CRP's mission is to:

- Inform citizens about how money in politics affects their lives.
- Empower voters and activists by providing unbiased information.
- Advocate for a transparent and responsive government.

Action Plan: Refuse to Contribute to Congress, Instead Fund a Citizens' Revolt

You need to reconsider donating to any congressional candidate unless they've been "vetted" on where they stand on issues that are important to their constituents, as well as whether their legislative efforts/votes have been compromised by campaign contributions.

Instead, contribute to those who intend to clean up Washington.

Here's where you can make an online donation to Accountability Now: http://www.actblue.com/page/accountabilitynow.

Here's where you contribute to the Center for Responsive Politics: https://secure.groundspring.org/dn/index.php?aid=17127.

The Big Fix: Recruit the Smartest Workers from Around the World, Send Most Kids to College, Measure Household Wealth

Along with putting the business lobby out of business, we've got to act as though we're preparing for a global economic Olympics.

We've seen how the decline of the union movement and a lack of a citizens' PAC means that most Americans can't afford to retire. We learned how the shrinking of government subsidies for college forces Americans to pay through the nose for it—at a point in history when most Americans need a degree to qualify for the best-paying jobs.

While the misdeeds I've recounted aren't capital crimes, they still cause a lot of suffering. How can managers of American companies justify cutting 401(k) matches or increasing co-pays on employee health coverage—or dropping it altogether—while simultaneously boosting executive pensions or executive health coverage? Or pressure their employees to lobby against legislation that would make it easier for them to start a union? How can colleges justify depriving students of the opportunity to consider the government's direct lending program or invading students' privacy by selling their contact information to the credit card companies? How about the management of rating agencies who misrepresented the soundness of securitized mortgage instruments, along with the brokers who approved borrowers for mortgages they couldn't afford—or the members of Congress who fought against or removed oversight over the mortgage industry?

Partisan Bickering Gets Us Nowhere

Along with confronting morally hazardous behavior that causes financial stress, America is suffering from political gridlock. As comedian Lewis Black famously put it, "The Republicans are the party of bad ideas and the Democrats of no ideas." While many might argue that the reverse is true today, the basic point remains valid. The Republican trickle-down economic remedies have failed us: tax incentives to save for retirement don't work because Americans aren't expected to be savers; only about 6% of the working population contributes to a deductible IRA. Republicans also suffer from innumeracy when it comes to "tax break" solutions for college costs: a 529 college savings plan of a few thousand dollars a year isn't going to buy your kids a $160,000 college education. In fact the very existence of 529 plans wasn't a result of consumer demand but very likely came about because the mutual fund industry lobbied to exempt earnings on these savings from taxes.

At the same time, the Democratic panacea of WPA-style government spending is equally wrong-headed, producing more bureaucrats, ineptitude, and boondoggles, rather than prosperity. What's more, the recent tax breaks supported by both parties sanction the counterintuitive notion that splurging at Wal-Mart is going to boost the wealth of American households, as opposed to that of Chinese manufacturers.

American Leaders Need to Eat Some Humble Pie

But our other failing is in not realizing that the U.S. is in danger of losing the "race to the top," as we compete for global market share in the high-paying, high-tech economy. We're essentially in denial over the fact that we are rapidly losing our status as the world's superpower. It isn't just General Motors that saw Toyota overtake it as the world's largest automaker, but increasingly companies from other countries are grabbing market share—from Nokia to Ikea. W. Edwards Deming, the quality control guru who taught the leaders of Japanese companies about quality management, said that when changes are gradual people don't notice them, and they assume that when hard times happen things will just return to normal by themselves if they just wait long enough—or apply outdated remedies. "We can only see the decline by looking back. A cat is unaware that dusk has settled upon the earth. Her pupils expand as light recedes but she is helpless as any of us in total darkness."

The New York Times columnist Thomas Friedman authored a best-selling book offering insights into the increasingly globalized world called *The World Is Flat*. But his revelations don't seem to have changed the way his colleagues cover foreign affairs. If anything is written about China in the *Times*, the stories typically reaffirm the stereotypes of intolerance of political dissent or the grinding poverty of those laid off from factory jobs. Somehow, they miss China's extraordinary emergence as a global superpower despite remaining a Communist regime—furthermore, a superpower that we must rely on to buy our Treasury bills.

Because of the lack of U.S. media coverage of China's meteoric rise, Americans are typically shocked when they visit the country for the first time; witness former Iowa governor Tom Vilsack's amazement on his first visit in 1999. SEIU President Andy Stern experienced similar culture shock in 2002 when his plane landed in Beijing for a meeting with union executives. "I discovered busy roadways...shimmering skyscrapers.... Beijing is now encircled by six highways, like Washington, D.C.'s beltway."

Stern acknowledges that too many union leaders are xenophobic, like America's political leadership. "American unions had a policy dating back to the Cold War of refusing to interact with 'government dominated' unions and would not recognize the ACFTU (All China Federation of Trade Unions) or speak officially to its leaders," he says. "I found that policy counterproductive. Most Fortune 500 companies have been investing madly in China. From around the world, professors, students, journalists, athletes, artists—and unions—travel to China in acknowledgment of its rapid emergence as a power player in all aspects of world affairs."

As Fareed Zakaria, editor of *Newsweek International*, points out, America's leaders have got to stop trying to boss other countries around and get more humble—as well as see what the U.S. can learn from other countries, whether it's adopting features of their health-care systems or pension systems, or maybe learning how to balance a budget like Germany has managed to do. "Americans rarely benchmark to global standards because they are sure that their way must be the best and most advanced," Zakaria writes.

Unfortunately, what's scary about these stressful economic times—as was the case before World War II—is that when times get tough, people often become isolationist instead of engaging in a vital dialogue that will lead us back to prosperous times. The last time we saw sustained "economic nationalism" was in the 1930s, when trade collapsed and many countries went their own way. Nationalism and populism combined to create fascist governments in Europe and Asia, followed by the outbreak of World War II. It took a generation for their economies to get back on track. We can't afford to wait that long.

Unfortunately, while the 2007 Pew Global Attitudes Survey showed a remarkable worldwide increase in positive views about free trade, of the 47 countries polled, the U.S. came in dead last; what's more, in the five years the survey has been conducted, no country has shown a greater drop-off in support than the United States.

A Lesson from Hoover: Protectionism Equals Shooting Your Economy in the Foot

Those who can't remember the past are condemned to repeat it, as the writer George Santayana observes. Isolationism essentially equals economic suicide, as we've seen during the Depression, when industries, including farmers, paraded before Congress demanding protection against "unfair" foreign competition, which is defined as competition that is willing and able to sell stuff for less than you do.

As a result, President Herbert Hoover enacted the Smoot-Hawley Tariff Bill, which raised rates sharply on agricultural and industrial products, on June 17, 1930, despite a petition opposing it signed by more than 1,000 economists. The consequences: other countries imposed their own higher tariffs in retaliation and world trade collapsed; American exports plummeted from $5.24 billion in 1929 to $1.6 billion in 1932, the lowest level since 1896.

Increase the "Supply of the Demand" of Highly Skilled Workers

The other dangerous protectionist tendency in tough economic times is to limit immigration. Unfortunately, a little-noticed provision in President Obama's stimulus package discourages banks that receive federal bailouts from hiring skilled foreign workers and foreshadows broader efforts to restrict work-related visa programs.

However, making it harder for immigrants to move here—whether they are Mexicans doing the jobs Americans are unwilling to do, or Indians working at highly skilled jobs—is the economic equivalent of shooting ourselves in the foot. Why do we need to encourage immigration? Because the solution to economic stress isn't for the same people to buy more stuff—especially since many Americans are over their heads in debt—but to increase the supply of workers who in turn buy stuff. In economic terms, we need to increase the "supply of the demand."

Canada not only has a regulated banking system, but it also has an immigration system that welcomes talented people rather than slamming the door in their faces. For example, while U.S. visas for skilled workers are capped at 85,000 a year and would-be immigrants from India and China wait close to six years because there are per-country caps of 10,000 or so, Canada has no such limits. Skilled workers can apply for a Canadian Skilled Worker Visa, which allows them to become "permanent residents"—no need for a sponsoring employer, or even a job.

Companies are noticing. In 2007, Microsoft, frustrated by its inability to hire foreign graduate students in the U.S., decided to open a research center in Vancouver. So the brightest Chinese and Indian engineers who are attracted to U.S. universities wind up being thrown out of the U.S. and picked up by Canada, where many of them will innovate and pay taxes for the rest of their lives.

America hasn't lost its status as a beacon of entrepreneurialism. Between 1996 and 2004, we created an average of 550,000 new small businesses **every month**. Net employment gains among surviving new firms in the 1990s typically grew by nearly 150% in the first two years of a U.S. start-up—compared to less than 50% for many European countries.

But as Zakaria points out, we need immigrant brains to work in these new businesses to stay competitive. Because our native-born, white American population has the same low birth rate as Europe's, without immigration U.S. GDP growth over the past quarter century would have been as low as Europe's. Immigrants account for 50% of the science researchers in this country, and half of all Silicon Valley start-ups have one founder who is an immigrant or first-generation American. In all, a quarter of America's science and technology start-ups, generating $52 billion in sales and employing 450,000 people, have had somebody born abroad as either their CEO or their CTO. In 2006, foreign nationals were named as inventors or co-inventors in 25% of American patent applications, nearly four times the 7.6% figure in 1998.

The Solution: 21st-Century Manhattan Projects and Better Education for a 21st-Century Workforce

While President Obama's emphasis on education is admirable—from preschool to "post-school"—his Keynesian approach to jump-starting the economy through tax cuts and public works projects may offer a short-term boost to construction jobs and keep store clerks on the job longer, but it isn't going to create skilled jobs at Microsoft or replace the jobs that IBM outsources to India.

Instead we should consider a two-pronged approach to getting the U.S. out of its economic doldrums: government-funded research on innovation that will result in high-paying jobs and education reform that will boost the number of Americans attending college so that they can work at these jobs.

John Kao, an expert on innovation who advises Fortune 500 business leaders, suggests we jump-start our economic advantage by developing 20 Innovation Hubs, at an initial cost of $20 billion, that would serve as bridge builders between right-brained creative industries and the left-brained mainstream, following models pioneered by the Learning Lab in Denmark and Arts & Business in the United Kingdom. Innovation research could be focused on digital media, clean technology, agricultural biotechnology, and nanomolecular materials, which enable researchers to build objects one atom or molecule at a time. For example, advanced organic solar cells could help solve our energy problems and molecular medicine could help doctors use less invasive techniques to diagnose and treat diseases.

Kao references the Manhattan Project, the Apollo Project, and Sematech as templates for success with a rapid turnaround time. In less than four years—1941 to 1945—the Manhattan Project successfully designed the atomic bomb and produced fissile materials for bombs. In less than 12 years after the Soviet Union's Sputnik spacecraft shocked the nation in 1957, the U.S. put a man on the moon. Thirty years later, concerned that Japanese companies were stealing market share in technology, the federal government joined with 14 U.S. semiconductor manufacturers to create Sematech, a manufacturing technology consortium. Seven years later, the project was successful enough that Sematech's board of directors voted to end its federal funding.

Raising the Bar on Education

Our need to raise our educational standards is the mission of the National Center on Education and the Economy (NCEE), which was launched in 1989. The NCEE created the Commission on the Skills of the American Workforce, which issued a report in 2006 that called for a dramatic redesign of the education system. The Commission called for setting up a standardized test that most students would take at the end of the 10th grade; students who scored well enough on the test would be guaranteed entrance to a community college to begin a program leading to either a two-year technical degree or the beginning of a four-year program completed at a state college. This approach accomplishes two tasks: getting kids focused on preparing for college earlier—as opposed to getting tutored on "goosing" their SAT scores—*and* taking a more affordable approach to getting a college degree.

The commission's other major recommendation is to recruit better teachers; too many currently come from the bottom third of their graduating class—most likely because the other two-thirds seek higher paying jobs in the private sector. The aim would be to pay beginning teachers about $45,000 a year, those working at the top of their career ladders about $95,000, and those who put in longer hours as much as $110,000. Again, many of our global competitors pay their teachers more. The Japanese, for instance, set teachers' pay by law at the top of the ranks for career civil servants; beginning teacher pay is about the same as it is for beginning engineers.

The exciting news is that President Obama takes education seriously, supporting not only making higher education more affordable by getting the private lenders out of the business but also raising standards in the public schools, something his predecessor tried to accomplish with limited success.

In a speech before the U.S. Hispanic Chamber of Commerce in early March of 2009, President Obama called for states to stop lowering testing standards, pushing for the No Child Left Behind Act to be more effectively tied to results. He denounced the practices of some states that "cheat" to have more of their kids pass the No Child Left Behind Test; for example, despite the fact that fourth-grade readers in Mississippi score 70 points worse than their peers in Wyoming, they receive the same grade.

In addition, Secretary of Education Arne Duncan is advocating lengthening the school year by having kids take classes in the summer. "When I go out and talk about that it doesn't always make me popular with the students," said Duncan to a reporter in February of 2009. But he pointed out that students in India and China—is it a coincidence that he picked these two countries?—go to school longer, which is why they are performing better.

Another good sign that President Obama is serious about education is his commitment to early childhood education, calling preschool a central piece of his domestic agenda. New Jersey Gov. Jon Corzine has also launched an ambitious plan to call on every district in the state to start providing all-day programs for low-income three- and four-year-olds by the fall of 2009; New Jersey is among 38 states with at least some state-funded programs.

Early childhood education doesn't simply give kids a head start on learning, it challenges the assumptions that preschoolers are too young to understand advanced concepts. My friend Nancy Faunce runs a company called FasTracKids, which has enabled a significant number of three- to six-year-old kids to improve their vocabulary and social skills at a rate 1½ times faster than their peers. Vocabulary is important because preschoolers' oral language achievements are critically linked with reading, academic, and social skills.

President Obama's Challenge: Measuring and Boosting Household Wealth
The Goal: Own, Don't Owe

U.S. economists should measure a country's wealth based on whether *what's owned* is on track to be much greater than *what's owed*. Specifically, we need to measure how these new initiatives in education and innovation, along with pension, mortgage, college cost, and credit card reform, are "promoting" members of the middle class to the upper middle class. As I mentioned in Chapter 2, President Obama has created the Middle Class Task Force—addressing shrinking healthcare coverage, job instability, affordable education, and retirement insecurity—and this office would be the perfect venue for overseeing these initiatives.

Unfortunately, the most closely monitored measure of America's economic growth is the level of consumer spending—not whether wages are growing based on an increased skill set required of a 21st century workforce. Also, the general measure of wealth is productivity, which is output divided by hours—not whether productivity is rewarded by higher wages, causing household wealth to rise relative to debt. Another concern is whether supply and demand are out of sync—that is, that there's not enough stuff for people who want to purchase stuff—not whether consumers are "demanding" more than they can afford.

What's more, as evidence of a lack of understanding of the effect of globalization, there is unjustified ongoing concern about inflation, despite the fact that inflation has been essentially killed by lower-wage countries such as India and China doing what we used to do. If you compare the rates of inflation during the first seven years of this decade, they average less than 3% as opposed to the 1970s, when they peaked at more than 13%, or the 1980s when they topped 12%. Why does this lack of insight matter? Because a Fed chairman who raises interest rates when he *thinks* inflation is rearing its ugly head isn't just showing a lack of understanding of what drives inflation, he's making borrowing more expensive.

While Ben Bernanke doesn't appear to be an advocate of the Milton Friedman school of "lawless enterprise" approach to managing the economy, as was the case with his predecessor, his seeming lack of understanding of economic stress is unsettling. His 2004 statement that home prices were "supported in very large part by strong fundamentals," including high incomes and low mortgage rates, is way off base, given that, when we factor in inflation, the median wage has actually gotten lower over the past two decades and that in 2004, the year he made the statement about low mortgage rates, then-Fed Chairman Alan Greenspan started a series of 17 interest-rate increases.

Create a Household Wealth Index

We may not be able to minimize the Fed's influence on economic policy, but there's no reason why President Obama can't commission the Fed to use its current research to measure household wealth.

Obama's Middle Class Task Force could monitor the success of these measures through a Household Wealth Index, which would be published annually and measure wage growth, 401(k) asset growth, the decrease in the percentage of income spent repaying student loan debt as well as increased healthcare coverage and lower employer per capita expenditures on it. It would also track the level of mortgage debt compared to incomes, including home-equity loans and the rate of cash-out mortgage refinancings, and the decrease in credit card debt. Factoring in student loan debt is particularly important; believe it or not, when the Federal Department of Education quantifies college tuition subsidies, it includes loans in the subsidies along with grants and aid—apparently unaware that loans increase the cost of education rather than lowering it.

The survey would be published annually, and it would be based on data collected in the private sector, such as Fidelity's and Vanguard's survey of 401(k) account balances. It would replace the Fed's Survey of Consumer Finances, which is a series of interviews with people—not a particularly scientific way to measure wealth, since few members of households know how much credit card debt they carry or how much money is in their 401(k) or rollover accounts.

We're facing the toughest economic challenge since the Great Depression but I believe we're up to it. Our nation of determined immigrants managed to defeat the Redcoats, abolish slavery, vanquish Adolph Hitler, and convince the Soviet Union to ditch Communism, not to mention achieving breakthroughs in medicine, science, and technology.

As a nation, we constantly defy expectations. Nearly 50 years ago, John F. Kennedy was considered a long shot for the presidency because he was a Catholic, then considered a radical religion by some Christians. Our current President was considered not only a long shot for the presidency—many black leaders thought the U.S. wasn't ready for a black President—but a long shot for the Senate seat he held earlier. As Obama would say on the presidential campaign trail, "I want to win...but I don't just want to win. I want to transform the country." I'm confident we will.

Endnotes

Introduction

1 Ronald Reagan narrative is from http://www.usnews.com/articles/news/politics/2008/01/17/the-actor-and-the-detail-man.html.

1 Narrative on average CEO wage is from "2008 Trends in CEO Pay," http://www.aflcio.org/corporatewatch/paywatch/pay/index.cfm.

1 Narrative on average weekly earnings is from the National Center for Education and the Economy, *Tough Choices for Tough Times*, New York, New York, John Wiley & Sons, Inc., 2007, p. 5.

2 Narrative on CNN Opinion Research Corp. poll is from http://www.cnn.com/2009/POLITICS/03/24/cafferty.economy/index.html.

2 Narrative on decline in pension plan coverage is from "The Decline of Private-Sector Defined Benefit Promises and Annuity Payments: What Will It Mean?" Employee Benefit Research Institute, Vol. 25, No. 7, July 2004, p. 2, 9.

4 Narrative about homeowners "underwater" is from Edmund L. Andrews and Lewis Uchitelle, "Rescues Weighed as Homeowners Wallow in Debt," *New York Times*, February 22, 2008, p. A1.

4 "I ask every American" quote is from http://www.whitehouse.gov/the_press_office/remarks-of-president-barack-obama-address-to-joint-session-of-congress/.

6 Narrative on number of lobbyists is from Center for Responsive Politics.

Chapter 1

9 AMP Financial Services narrative is from "The AMP Superannuation Adequacy Index Report," Access Economics Pty Limited, 2008.

9 Investment Company Institute narrative is from "U.S. Retirement Assets Hit $16.6 Trillion in First Quarter," Investment Company Institute, October 2007, http://www.ici.org/statements/nr/2007/07_q1_retmrkt_update.html.

10 Fidelity Investments narrative is from *Building Futures*, Vol. VIII, Fidelity Investments, p. 17.

10 Australian employer contribution rate is from Slide 5, PowerPoint presentation by Jane White at Filling Our Empty Nest Egg forum, New America Foundation, July 8, 2008.

10 Match suspension narrative is from "Companies That Have Changed or Temporarily Suspended Their 401(k) Matching Contributions," Pension Rights Center, February 7, 2009, http://www.pensionrights.org/pubs/facts/401(k)-match.html.

11 Australian over-50 contributions narrative is from National Information Centre on Retirement Investments, Inc., "A Super Guide," Woden, Australia, January 7, 2007, p. 17.

11 Narrative on baby boomer Australians selling a home is from Slide 5, Op. Cit.

11 Narrative on Australians contributing more to their accounts than their employers is from Anna Fenech, "Individuals' Super Contributions Beat Those of Employers," *The Australian*, September 28, 2007, p. 23.

11 Narrative on U.S. pension generosity versus other countries is from Organization for Economic Cooperation and Development, *Pensions at a Glance: Public Policies Across OECD Countries*, Paris, France, OECD, 2007, p. 49.

12 Australia is one of eight countries narrative is from ibid., p. 25.

12 Denmark's is 11.8% narrative is from ibid., p. 28–30.

12 Average CEO wage narrative is from Anderson, Sarah, Pizzigati, Sam, "Workers Need Added Clout to Close the Pay Gap with CEOs," September 1, 2008 http://www.ips-dc.org/articles/658 13.

12 Average weekly earnings narrative is from National Center for Education and the Economy, *Tough Choices for Tough Times*, New York, New York, John Wiley & Sons, Inc., 2007, p. 5.

12 Now it's $7.7 million narrative is from http://www.aflcio.org/corporate-watch/pay/index.cfm.

13 Mercer narrative is from PricewaterhouseCoopers, "2007/2008 US Human Capital Effectiveness Report," 2007, p. 5.

14 Narrative on decline in coverage is from "The Decline of Private-Sector Defined Benefit Promises and Annuity Payments: What Will It Mean?" Employee Benefit Research Institute, Vol. 25, No. 7, July 2004, p. 2, 9.

14 Narrative on ERISA being amended is from http://law.freeadvice.com/insurance_law/insurance_law/erisa-law.htm.

14 Narrative on terminations is from Michael Shari, and Virginia Munger-Kahn, "Money Management—Dead Plan Walking," *Institutional Investor*, May 2007, p. 1.

14 Narrative on the 1980s is from ibid.

15 Narrative on contributions to pension plans is from ibid.

15 Narrative on Pension Protection Act is from ibid.

15 Quote from Thomas Donlan is from Thomas G. Donlan, "How Much Pension Reform?," *Barron's*, New York, August 14, 2006, p. 39.

15 Narrative on more than 1,200 employers is from http://www.usnews.com/blogs/planning-to-retire/2009/01/02/over-1000-companies-have-recently-eliminated-employee-pensions.html.

16 Quote from Robert Reich is from Robert Reich, *Supercapitalism*, Alfred. A. Knopf, 2007, p. 67.

16 Narrative on fiduciary requirements is from http://www.dol.gov/elaws/ ebsa/fiduciary/q.46b.htm.

16 Computer model narrative is from http://www.financial-planning.com/ news/new-rules-retirement-advice-mixed-reviews-2661415-1.html.

17 Changes jobs every four years narrative is fromhttp://www.economist .com/daily/chartgallery/displaystory.cfm?story_id=9934771.

17 Narrative on Ted Benna is from "Father of 401(k) Says Intent Was Different," *Centre Daily Times*, State College, PA, October 27, 2007.

17 David Wray quote is from http://seattletimes.nwsource.com/html/ businesstechnology/2002164599_pfretirement30.html.

19 Narrative on contribution rates is from Jane White's testimony before the Working Group on Financial Literacy on September 19, 2007.

20 Quote from Investment Company Institute is from Jillian Mincer, "As the 401(k) Turns 25, Has It Improved with Age?" *The Wall Street Journal*, November 14, 2006, p. D2.

21 Narrative on Retirement Income Indicator is from Fidelity Investments, Op. Cit., p. 2.

21 "Broadly successful" quote from Vanguard Group is from Vanguard Group, "How America Saves 2008," p. 7.

21 Vanguard description of auto-enrollment is from ibid., p. 26.

21 T. Rowe contribution rate narrative is from "T. Rowe Retirement Plan Services," 2005, p. 2.

22 Vanguard calculator narrative is from Vanguard—Saving for Retirement, "How Much Should I Save for Retirement?" August 28, 2007, https:// personal.vanguard.com/VGApp/hnw/RetirementSavings.

22 Narrative on Fidelity's calculator is from http://personal.fidelity.com/planning/retirement/plan-overview.shtml.cvsr?refpr=rcc18

22 Quote from Michael Clowes is from Employee Benefit Research Institute, Op. Cit., p. 5.

22 The waking-up-rich narrative is from E. S. Browning and Stephen E.Frank, "Waking Up Rich: Retirement Accounts Stashed in Stocks Make Employees Millionaires—Workers, Often Just Lucky, See the 401(k) Statement and Start Making Plans—A Sailboat, Poetry and Zen," *The Wall Street Journal*, New York, July 7, 1997, p. A1.

23 Ted Benna quote is from Ted Benna, "Don't Alter 401(k) Funding: Millionaires Are Rare and Most People Save Too Little," *Compensation and Benefits Review*, Saranac Lake, November/December 1997, p. 66.

24 Narrative on 20-year-holding periods is from author research based on *Stocks, Bonds, Bills and Inflation, 2007 Yearbook*, Morningstar, Inc.

25 Narrative on Ghilarducci proposal is from Teresa Ghilarducci, "Save Pensions" (Op-Ed), *New York Times*, New York, September 27, 2008, p. 21.

26 Alicia Munnell narrative is from Alicia Munnell, *Working Longer*, Washington, D.C., Brookings Institution Press, 2008, p. 5.

26 A 3% starting rate narrative is from Jane White, "Filling America's Nest Eggs," White Paper, January 2008, p. 13.

27 Auto-enrollment and Plansponsor and Vanguard narrative is from Eleanor Laise, "Automatic 401(k) Plans Might Not Save Enough," *The Wall Street Journal*, January 9, 2008, p. D3.

27 Direct deposit IRA narrative is from http://www.bloomberg.com/apps/news?pid=2060123&refer=home&sid=a1.x9_d3sPcO.

28 "As Boomers Retire" narrative is from Ian MacDonald, "Golden Years: As Boomers Retire, Insurers Aim to Cash In," *The Wall Street Journal*, June 15, 2007, p. A1.

28 Introduction of Retirement Security for Life Act narrative (Jones and English) is from "Retirement Security for Life Act of 2007 and Its Potential Effect on Annuities," InsuranceNewsNet.com, Inc., June 29, 2007.

29 Gordon Smith sponsorship of act is from "Retirement Security for Life Act Introduced in Senate by Sen. Smith," US Fed News Service, April 16, 2007.

29 NASD Investor Alert narrative is from "Commentary: Some Early Retirement Investment Pitches Promise Too Much," *Regional Business News*, December 4, 2006.

29 Florida annuity narrative is from Trevor Thomas, "Fla. Toughens Standards for Annuity," *National Underwriter*, July 21, 2008, p. 18-19.

30 Hartford Financial Services Group narrative is from "Hartford Admits Misconduct in Annuities Probe," HT Media Ltd., May 10, 2006.

30 New Jersey initiative narrative is from Jeff D. Opdyke, "Annuity Sales Face Crackdown by Regulators; As Complaints Rise, New Laws Seek to Improve Risk Disclosure and Ease Withdrawal Penalties," *The Wall Street Journal*, August 4, 2005, p. D1.

32 Australians who earn less narrative is from PowerPoint presentation by Jane White, Op. Cit.

Chapter 2

37 Quote from Arthur Levitt is from Arthur Levitt, *Take on the Street*, New York, New York, Pantheon Books, 2002, p. 17.

37 Take the stock market swoon narrative originally appeared in the *Employee Benefit News* column "Know When to Hold 'Em," July 2007.

38 In the 18 calendar years narrative is from *Stocks, Bonds, Bills and Inflation; Market Results for 1926-2006*, Morningstar, 2007, p. 36-37.

38 Depression narrative is from ibid.

38 Investors who missed the 40 best days narrative is from AIG VALIC Overview, http://www.aigvalic.com/fpc2003/uofa.nsf/contents/overview_is3. Page no longer available.

38 Go out even further narrative is from theGoodSteward.com, http://www.thegoodsteward.com/article.php3?articleID=418. Page no longer available.

39 Roth narrative originally appeared in *Employee Benefit News*, "The Roth 401(k): Because It's Not Nice to Tax Skimpy Nest Eggs," November 2006.

39 Twenty two percent narrative is from http://www.psca.org/MEDIA/PressReleases/tabid/97/ctl/detail/mid/475/id/39/Archive/Default.aspx.

43 Target date narrative originally appeared as "Target Practice," *Employee Benefit News*, May 1, 2007.

43 60% of 401(k) participants is from How America Saves, p. 4

43 International fund narrative originally appeared as "If They Can't Beat Globalization, 401(k) Investors Need to Profit from It," *Employee Benefit News*, January 2008.

43 Only one-third of participants narrative is from How America Saves 2008, Op. Cit., p. 36.

46 Task Force narrative is from http://blogs.suntimes.com/sweet/2008/12/obama_white__house_task_force_o.html.

47 Employees working in companies narrative is from Michael Calabrese, A Universal 401(k).

47 Narrative on Baby Boomer Australians selling a home is from Slide 5, PowerPoint presentation by Jane White at Filling Our Empty Nest Egg forum, New America Foundation, July 8, 2008.

47 Disclose necessary co-pay narrative is from Jane White, "Filling America's Empty Nest Eggs," p. 22.

48 Twenty percent narrative is from ibid., p. 5.

48 Eight percent of employees narrative is from How America Saves, Op. Cit., p. 5.

51 Cautious approach narrative is from http://www.opensecrets.org/payback/issue.php?issueid=PR1&CongNo=107.

51 In a letter to Sen. Max Baucus narrative is from a July 1, 2002 letter signed by the Coalition on Employee Retirement Benefits Steering Committee.

51 House Education and Labor Committee narrative is from http://www.opensecrets.org/cmteprofiles/overview.php?comteid=H08&cmte=HEDU&cogno=110&chamber=H.

52 House Ways and Means Committee narrative is from http://www.opensecrets.org/cmteprofiles/overview.php?comteid=H22&cmte=HEDU&cogno=110&chamber=H.

Chapter 3

55 Median sales price narrative is from "Median Sales Price of Existing Single-Family Homes," National Association of Realtors.

55 Narrative about couple buying home near San Francisco is from Peter Coy, Rich Miller, and Lauren Young, "Is a Housing Bubble About to Burst?" *Business Week*, July 19, 2004, p. 36-37.

55 Narrative about families in Los Angeles is from Barbara E. Hernandez, "Few Households Can Buy in East Bay: 9.3% of Families Can Afford Homes in the Region, Ranked as the 19th Least Affordable by a Trade Group," *Contra Costa Times*, February 23, 2007.

56 Narrative about couple who couldn't afford their home is from Stephen Gandel, Amanda Gengler, and Paul Keegan, "For Sale: Scenes from a Bubble," *Money*, May 2007, p. 114-121.

57 Narrative about homeowners underwater is from Edmund L. Andrews and Louis Uchitelle, "Rescues Weighed as Homeowners Wallow in Debt," *New York Times*, February 22, 2008, p. A1.

58 Narrative on the Depository Institutions Deregulation and Money Control Act is from Richard Bitner, *Confessions of a Subprime Lender*, New York, New York, John Wiley & Sons, Inc., 2008, p. 23.

58 Until the 1980s narrative is from Greg Ip, and Damien Paletta, "Lending Oversight: Regulators Scrutinized in Mortgage Meltdown; States, Federal Agencies Clashed on Subprimes as Market Ballooned," March 22, 2007, p. A1.

59 Narrative about government subsidies is from Shirley L. Benzler, "Housing: A Spark of Life," *The New York Times*, June 22, 1975.

60 Narrative on rent control is from ibid.

60 Narrative on housing secretary is from "Housing Secretary Names Task Force on New-Home Price," August 27, 1977, *Chicago Tribune*, p. B7.

60 Narrative on America's new Levittowns is from Robert Lindsey, "America's New Levittowns," *The New York Times*, July 6, 1980.

60 Narrative on Ronald Reagan is from Andy Zipser, "Gimme Shelter (A Special Report): Extremes—Broken Promises: Low-Cost Housing Stock Shrinks Even as the Need for It Grows," *The Wall Street Journal*, May 19, 1989, p. 1.

60 Unemployment rate is from U.S. Department of Labor, Bureau of Labor Statistics, Labor Force Statistics from the Current Population Survey.

60 Narrative on income adjusted for inflation is from Matthew L. Wald, "Americans Want to Own a Home, Despite Rising Cost," *The New York Times*, February 28, 1985, p. C1.

61 Narrative on Alan Greenspan is from Neil Irwin, Amit R. Paley, "Greenspan Says He Was Wrong on Regulation; Lawmakers Blast Former Fed Chairman," October 24, 2008, P. A1.

61 Narrative on Bernanke's confirmation hearings is from David Leonhardt, "Pushing Fed to Act Early If Not Often," *The New York Times*, August 22, 2007, p. C1.

61 Quote from Bernanke is from John Cassidy, "Anatomy of a Meltdown," *New Yorker*, December 2008, p. 49-63.

62 Narrative on nearly 1 million jobs is from Robyn Meredith, "The Elephant and the Dragon," W.W. Norton & Co., New York, 2007–8, Kindle Edition, location 3414–20.

62 In 2006 Bernanke predicted narrative is from http://www.blomberg.com/apps/news?pid=10000103&sid=abDkwDoUXJqs&refer=news_index.

62 Narrative on interest-only loans is from Kristin Downey, "Many Buyers Opt for Risky Mortgages; High Rate of Interest-Only Loans a Concern in Virginia," *The Washington Post*, May 28, 2005, p. A01.

63 Narrative on loans are attractive is from ibid.

63 Quote from Alan Fishbein is from ibid.

63 Quote from George Hanzimanolis is from *Money*, May 2007, Op. Cit.

63 Narrative on appraisers feeling pressure is from Jonathan D. Epstein, "Appraisers Feel Pressure to Inflate Home Estimates," *Buffalo News*, June 13, 2005.

Chapter 4

67 Narrative on OCC and SEC is from Paul Beckett and Jess Bravin, "Friendly Watchdog: Federal Regulator Often Helps Banks Fighting Consumers—Dependent on Lender's Fees, OCC Takes Their Side Against Local, State Laws—Defending Uniform Rules," *The Wall Street Journal*, January 28, 2002, p. A1.

68 Narrative on National Bank Act is from ibid.

68 Narrative on attorneys general from North Carolina, etc., is from Robert Berner and Brian Grow, "They Warned Us," *Business Week*, October 20, 2008, p. 36.

68 Keest quote is from ibid.

68 Roy Barnes narrative is from ibid.

69 Frank Jackson narrative is from ibid.

70 Phil Gramm narrative is from Michael Hirsh, "The Predators' Ball; Fannie Mae and Freddie Mac Have Helped Defang Laws That Might Have Prevented the Subprime Mess," *Newsweek*, August 25, 2008.

71 AIG narrative is from Bill Saporito, "How AIG Became Too Big to Fail," *Time*, March 30, 2009, p. 24.

71 Christopher Cox narrative is from ibid.

72 SEC revolving door narrative is from David Einhorn and Michael Lewis, "The End of the Financial World as We Know It," *The New York Times*, January 4, 2009, p. 9-10.

72 Henry Paulson narrative is from Stephen Labaton, "Agency's '04 Rule Let Banks Pile Up New Debt and Risk," *The New York Times*, October 3, 2008, p. A1.

73 Whitney National Bank narrative is from Mike McIntire, "Bailout Is a No-Strings Windfall to Bankers, If Not to Borrowers," *The New York Times*, January 18, 2009, p. A1.

73 Refinancing narrative is from James R. Hagerty and Ruth Simon, "Rates Fall, but Refinancings Are Limited," *The Wall Street Journal*, January 15, 2009, p. A2.

73 Obama foreclosure incentive plan narrative is from Edmund L. Andrews, "U.S. Sets Big Incentives to Head Off Foreclosures," *The New York Times*, March 5, 2009, p. A1.

74 World Economic Forum and over-leveraged narrative is from Fareed Zakaria, "Worthwhile Canadian Initiative; Canadian Banks Are Typically Leveraged at 18 to 1—Compared with U.S. Banks at 26 to 1," *Newsweek*, February 16, 2009.

74 Canadian median home price narrative is from the Canadian Real Estate Association, www.crea.ca/public/news_stats/statistics.htm; various U.S. cities narrative is from "National Association of REALTORS Median Sales Price of Existing Single-Family Homes for Metropolitan Areas."

74 Narrative on weekly or biweekly payments is from Holloway, Andy, "Safe as Houses," Canadian Business, 4/28/2008, p. 42-45. Op. Cit.

75 Mid-June 2009 narrative is from Damien Paletta, "Historic Overhaul of Finance rules," *The Wall Street Journal*, June 18, P 1.

75 Insurgents narrative is from Michael Hirsh, "The Insurgents: The Secret Battle to Save Capitalism," *Newsweek*, June 22, p. 44.

78 Narrative on Finance/Insurance/Real Estate is from http://www.opensecrets.org/indusries/indus.php?ind=F.

79 Narrative on National Association of Realtors is from http://www.opensecrets.org/orgs/index.php.

79 Narrative on Richard Shelby is from http://www.opensecrets.org/news/2008/05/housing-law-in-hands-of-senato.html.

Chapter 5

Portland

89 What you'll love about Portland narrative is from http://www.frommers. com/destinations/portlandor/0025010001.html.

90 Major employers narrative is from Portland Business Alliance & Commerce, December 2007.

90 Climate narrative is from "Portland Airport Climate & Weather— Airports Guide to Portland," http://www.portland-pdx.airports-guides. com/pdx_climate.html.

90 Summertime Concerts at Oregon Zoo narrative is from Karl Samson, *Frommer's Portable Portland*, 5th ed., p. 3.

90 The Arlene Schnitzer Concert Hall narrative is from ibid., p. 2.

90 Berbati's Pan narrative is from ibid., p. 119.

90 The Japanese Garden narrative is from ibid., p. 2.

90 Driving and Hiking on the Gorge narrative is from ibid.

90 Wine Tasting in the Nearby Wine Country narrative is from ibid., p. 3.

90 The Annual Portland Pirate Festival narrative is from http://www. frommers.com/destinations/portlandor/0025010021.html.

90 Oregon Museum of Science and Industry narrative is from Karl Samson, Op. Cit., p. 8.

90 Virtual Parachuting narrative is from ibid., p. 9.

Denver

91 What you'll love about Denver narrative is from "Denver Travel Guide," http://www.fodors.com/world/north-america/usa/colorado/denver/ and "About Denver: Facts & Info," http://www.denver.org/metro.

92 Major employers narrative is from Metro Denver EDC, April 2008.

92 Climate narrative is from "Denver Airport Climate & Weather—
Airports Guide to Denver," http://www.denver-den.airports-guides.
com/den_climate.html.

92 Denver March Pow Wow narrative is from http://events.frommers.com/
sisp/frommers2/index.htm?fx=guide&frommers_id=7.

92 Vans Warped Tour narrative is from http://events.frommers.com/sisp/
frommers2/index.htm?fx=guide&frommers_id=7.

92 Denver Botanic Gardens narrative is from Denver Travel Guide, Op. Cit.

92 Winter Park Resort narrative is from http://www.denver.org/metro/
features/ski-denver.

92 Loveland Ski Area narrative is from http://www.denver.org/metro/
features/ski-denver.

San Antonio

93 What you'll love about San Antonio narrative is from "San Antonio
Travel Guide," http://www.fodors.com/world/north-america/usa/texas/
san-antonio/more.html.

94 Major employers narrative is from "Guide to Military Installations,"
2008, and "San Antonio Business Journal Book of Lists," 2008.

94 Climate narrative is from "San Antonio Airport Climate & Weather—
Airports Guide to San Antonio," http://www.san-antonio-sat.airports-
guides.com/sat_climate.html.

94 The Alameda narrative is from http://www.fodors.com/world/north-
america/usa/texas/san-antonio/review-434554.html.

94 Luminaria Arts Night in San Antonio narrative is from http://www.
visitsanantonio.com/visitors/play/festivals-events/index.aspx.

94 Juneteenth narrative is from http://www.visitsanantonio.com/visitors/play/festivals-events/index.aspx.

94 Mitchell Lake narrative is from http://www.fodors.com/world/north-america/usa/texas/san-antonio/activity_2109734.html.

94 Natural Bridge Caverns narrative is from http://www.fodors.com/world/north-america/usa/texas/san-antonio/activity_2109734.html.

94 The Witte Museum narrative is from http://www.visitsanantonio.com/visitors/play/attractions-rundown/index.aspx.

Austin

95 What you'll love about Austin narrative is from Fodor's Web site, "Austin Travel Guide," http://www.fodors.com/world/north-america/usa/texas/austin/more.html.

96 Major employers narrative is from "Austin Business Journal Book of Lists," 2008, and Greater Austin Chamber of Commerce, April 2007.

96 Climate narrative is from "Austin Airport Climate & Weather—Airports Guide to Austin," http://www.austin-aus.airports-guides.com/aus_climate.html.

96 Culture narrative is from http://www.frommers.com/destinations/austin/0003010001.html.

96 Carnaval Brasileiro narrative is from http://events.frommers.com/sisp/index.htm?fx=event&event_id=28316.

96 Rock Climbing narrative is from http://www.frommers.com/destinations/austin/0003010020.html.

96 Spelunking narrative is from http://www.frommers.com/destinations/austin/0003010020.html.

96 Champion Park narrative is from http://www.fodors.com/world/north-america/usa/texas/austin/review-434825.html.

96 Edward's Aquifer narrative is from http://www.frommers.com/destinations/austin/A7744.html.

96 Zilker Zephyr Miniature Train narrative is from http://www.frommers.com/destinations/austin/A7745.html.

Houston

97 What you'll love about Houston narrative is from http://www.visithoustontexas.com/media/Houston_Descriptions.

98 Major employers narrative is from "Houston Business Journal Book of Lists," 2008, and *Houston Chronicle*, April 2007.

98 Climate narrative is from "Houston Airport Climate & Weather—Airports Guide to Houston," http://www.houston-hou.airports-guides.com/hou_climate.html.

98 CaribFest Carnival narrative is from http://events.frommers.com/sisp/index.htm?fx=event&event_id=40630.

98 Ballunar Liftoff Festival narrative is from http://events.frommers.com/sisp/index.htm?fx=event&event_id=41662.

98 Art Car Weekend narrative is from http://events.frommers.com/sisp/index.htm?fx=event&event_id=40490.

98. The Chevron Houston Marathon narrative is from http://events.frommers.com/sisp/index.htm?fx=event&event_id=100403.

98 Gulf Greyhound Park narrative is from http://www.visithoustontexas.com/visitors/sports/listing.details.php?category=12700&id=23022.

99 The Houston Children's Festival narrative is from http://events.frommers.com/sisp/index.htm?fx=event.search&sort=DATE&loc_id=132900&page=2.

99 Splashtown narrative is from http://www.guestlife.com/media/GuestLife/Houston/Annual-2008/HN08-Houston-Attractions-Guide/.

99 Kemah Boardwalk narrative is from http://www.guestlife.com/media/
    GuestLife/Houston/Annual-2008/HN08-Houston-Attractions-Guide/.

Raleigh

99 What you'll love about Raleigh narrative is from "Raleigh-Durham with
    Chapel Hill Travel Guide," http://www.fodors.com/world/north-america/
    usa/north-carolina/raleigh-durham-with-chapel-hill/.

100 Major employers narrative is from "Triangle Business Journal Book of
     Lists," 2009, and Wake County Economic Development, February 2006.

100 Climate narrative is from "Raleigh Airport Climate & Weather—
     Airports Guide to Raleigh," http://www.raleigh-rdu.airports-guides.
     com/rdu_climate.html.

100 Time Warner Cable Music Pavilion at Walnut Creek narrative is from
     http://events.frommers.com/sisp/index.htm?fx=event&event_id=145517.

100 Artsplosure narrative is from ibid.

100 William B. Umstead State Park narrative is from ibid., p. 122.

100 Capital City Bicycle Motocross Race Track narrative is from
     http://www.visitraleigh.com/visitors/listing.details.php?partner=14853&
     name=Capital+City+Bicycle+Motocross+Race+Track.

101 Adventure Landing narrative is from http://www.visitraleigh.com/
     visitors/listing.details.php?partner=14909&name=Adventure+Landing.

Chapter 6

105 Obamas often say narrative is from R. Gibson, J. McCormick, and C.
     Parsons, "How Broke Were Obamas? Hard to Tell," *Chicago Tribune*,
     April 20, 2008, p. 21.

105 In 1958 narrative is from "Going Broke By Degree/Why College Costs
     So Much," The AEI Press, Washington D.C. 2004, p. 8.

105 A generation ago narrative is from ibid., p. 26.

106 Freaks, brats narrative is from Steven V. Roberts, "Ronald Reagan Is Giving 'Em Heck," New York Times, October 25, 1970.

106 Federal budget narrative is from Anya Kamenetz, *Generation Debt*, New York, Riverhead Books, 2006, p. 26.

106 Of the 30 OECD countries narrative is from Ryan Hahn, "The Global State of Higher Education and the Rise of Private Finance," Institute for Higher Education Policy, 2007.

106 Tuition in France narrative is from "Vive la difference," *The Economist*, May 9-15, 2009, p. 29.

107 Our share of the world narrative is from is from National Center on Education and the Economy, *Tough Choices or Tough Times*, New York, John Wiley & Sons, Inc., 2007, p. xvi.

107 This fact is not lost on President Obama narrative is from http://www. whitehouse.gov/the_press_office/remarks-of-president-barack-obama-address-to-joint-session-of-congress/.

107 A poll of likely voters narrative is from Goldie Blumenstyk, "The $375-Billion Question: Why Does College Cost So Much?" *The Chronicle of Higher Education*, October 3, 2008.

108 The U.S. will need to be narrative is from Tough Choices or Tough Times, p. xxi.

108 U.S. manufacturing jobs vanished narrative is from Stephen Manning, "Is Anything Made in the U.S.A. Anymore?" *International Herald Tribune*, February 20, 2009.

108 Outsourcing poses a threat to America's middle-class jobs narrative is from "Who's in the Middle?" *The Economist*, February 14, 2009, p. 4.

109 Wage deflator narrative is from Fareed Zakaria, *The Post-American World*.

109 Tom Vilsack quote is from Scott Lehigh, "Help for the Democrats," *Boston Globe*, May 13, 2005.

110 U.S. math score narrative is from Walter Isaacson, "How to Raise the Standards in America's Schools," *Time*, April 27, 2009, p. 35 (source National Governors Association: nga.org/files/pdf/0812/benchmarking. pdf).

110 China and India's economies racing us to the top narrative is from *Tough Choices or Tough Times*, Op. Cit., p. 9.

110 Secondary schools in India narrative is from ibid., p. 11.

110 The story in China narrative is from ibid.

111 Record 76 colleges narrative is from Anonymous, "Rich Colleges, Poor Students," *The Christian Science Monitor*, January 30, 2008, p. 8.

111 The assets of Harvard's endowment narrative is from Glenn Beck, "Commentary: Tax-Free Hypocrisy from Higher Education," *CNN*, May 15, 2008.

111 In February of 2008 narrative is from Peter Schworm, "Colleges Guard Soaring Endowments: Many Resist Congressional Pressure to Curb Tuition Hikes, Offer More Aid," *Boston Globe*, February 28, 2008, p. A1.

111 Harvard and Williams College narrative is from Anne Marie Chacker, "Some Colleges Cut, Eliminate Student Debt; Soaring Tuition, Pressure to Spend Endowments Spur Schools to Offer More Grants," *The Wall Street Journal*, November 29, 2007, p. D1.

111 Wesleyan narrative is from March 14, 2008, letter to Wesleyan graduate from President Michael S. Roth.

112 Just 8.1% of Harvard's undergrads narrative is from Karin Fischer, "Elite Colleges Lag in Serving the Needy," *The Chronicle of Higher Education*, May 12, 2006, p. A1, A2.

Chapter 7

115 Narrative on *60 Minutes* is from Leslie Stahl, "Sallie Mae's Success Too Costly?" CBS News, May 7, 2006, http://www.cbsnews.com/stories/2006/05/05/60minutes/main1591583.shtml.

115 Collinge and Sallie Mae narrative is from ibid.

116 Bankruptcy narrative is from Ralph Nader, "Sallie Mae and the Student Loan Swindle," *Counter Punch*, May 13-14, 2006, http://www.counterpunch.org/nader05132006.html.

116 College costs in England narrative is from Mike Baker, "What University Is Going to Cost," BBC News, August 5, 2005, http://news.bbc.co.uk/go/pr/fr/-/1/hi/education/4749575.stm.

116 Lord and Fitzpatrick compensation narrative is from Albert B. Crenshaw, "Student Loans Are Private Affairs; Sallie Mae Cleaned Up When It Cut Public Ties," *The Washington Post*, November 22, 2004, p. E01.

117 Washington Nationals narrative is from Thomas Heath and David Nakamura, "Baseball Bidders Malek, Zients Meet with Selig," *The Washington Post*, October 20, 2005, p. B03.

117 Golf course narrative is from Daniel deVise, "Seeing Hazards: A Rich, New Landowner in Rural Arundel Wants a Personal Golf Course. But Is That All?" *The Washington Post*, January 27, 2006, p. B01.

117 Starting in the 1960s narrative is from "Student Loan Scandal," *The Washington Post*, September 10, 2004, p. A28.

118 Narrative on when the government established is from Eric Dash and Peter Edmonston, "Sallie Mae, Mired in Controversy," *The New York Times*, April 16, 2007, p. C1.

118 Sallie Mae quickly became narrative is from ibid.

119 When Congress tightened narrative is from ibid.

119 Opportunity loan narrative is from Julian E. Barnes, Megan Barnett, and Danielle Knight, "Big Money on Campus in the Multibillion-Dollar World of Student Loans, Big Lenders Are Finding New Ways to Drain Uncle Sam's Coffers," *U.S. News & World Report*, October 27, 2003, p. 30-40.

119 Planned interest rate reduction narrative is from ibid.

120 Guest of Albert Lord narrative is from Stephen Burd, "The Congressman and Sallie Mae," *Chronicle of Higher Education*, Vol. 52, Issue 21, January 27, 2006, p. A23-A24.

120 Loan-industry official narrative is from ibid.

120 Provision in the bill narrative is from ibid.

120 Trusted hands quote is from ibid.

121 Shays quote is from ibid.

121 Nelnet narrative is from William McQuillen, "Senate Report Details Relationships Between Student Lenders, Colleges," *The Washington Post*, September 5, 2007, p. D3.

121 Andrew Cuomo narrative is from Paul Basken and Kelly Field, "Student-Loan Investigation Sweeps Up More Colleges," *The Chronicle of Higher Education*, April 2007, p. A1.

121 Call center narrative is from Amit R. Paley and Tomoeh Murakami Tse, "Student Loan Giant Sallie Mae Settles in N.Y. Conflict-of-Interest Probe," *The Washington Post*, April 12, 2007, p. A1.

121 Luke Swarthout quote is from ibid.

122 Study abroad narrative is from Diana Jean Schemo, "In Study Abroad, Gifts and Money for Universities," *The New York Times*, August 13, 2007, p. A1.

123 Letter from George Miller and Barney Frank narrative is from Kelly Field, "House Democrats Question Timing of Sallie Mae Chief's Stock Sale," *The Chronicle of Higher Education*, June 2007, p. A22.

123 Lord quote is from David S. Hilzenrath, "Bad Loans Help Push Sallie Mae to Loss; Student Lender Concedes It Made Poor Decisions," *The Washington Post*, January 24, 2008, p. D1.

123 Worst CEO narrative is from Herb Greenberg, "The Buzz— MarketWatch Weekend Investor: 'Worst CEOs of Year—of 2008, That Is,'" *The Wall Street Journal*, January 5, 2008, p. B3.

123 Scuttled buyout narrative is from Michael de la Merced and Andrew Ross Sorkin, "Sallie Mae Settles Suit over Buyout That Fizzled," *The New York Times*, January 28, 2008, p. C1.

124 Spellings quote is from http://www.ed.gov/students/college/aid/loans.html.

124 Melissa Wagoner quote is from David S. Hilzenrath, "Administration Unveils Plan to Protect Student Lenders," *The Washington Post*, May 22, 2008, p. D1.

125 College Cost Reduction and Access Act narrative is from Randy Barrett, "Cap and Frown," *National Journal*, July 12, 2008, p. 44.

125 Then in August of 2008 narrative is from Tamar Lewin, "Congress Overhauls College Loan Regulations," *The New York Times*, August 1, 2008, p. A17.

125 In February of 2009 narrative is from Jonathan Glater, "Big Changes on the Way in Lending to Students," *New York Times*, February 27, 2009.

125 Pell Grant narrative is from http://www.cnn.com/2009/POLITICS/03/10/obama.education/index.html.

127 Sydney Frank narrative is from http://us.cnn.com/2009/LIVING05/25/brown.gradutes.sidney.frank.index.html.

128 Research conducted for author by Center for Responsive Politics.

Chapter 8

129 Bethany McLean, Sallie Mae narrative is from Alan Michael Collinge, *The Student Loan Scam: The Most Oppressive Debt in U.S. History— and How We Can Fight Back*, Boston, MA, Beacon Press, 2009, p. 99.

130 Clinton, Durbin narrative is from ibid., p. 101.

130 Education Department can now seize narrative is from John Hechinger, "College Try: U.S. Gets Tough on Failure to Repay Student Loans; Education Department Wields Heavy Hand, Critics Say, in Some Hard-Luck Cases; No Breaks in Bankruptcy Court," *The Wall Street Journal*, January 6, 2005, p. A1.

132 Need-based, merit-based, and other grants narrative is from Mark Kantrowitz and Doug Hardy, *FastWeb! College Gold: The Step-by-Step Guide to Paying for College*, 1st ed., New York, New York, HarperCollins Publishers, 2006, p. 8.

133 Narrative on articulation agreement in some states is from ibid., p. 243.

133 Narrative on four-year community colleges is from Tamar Lewin, "Community Colleges Challenge Hierarchy with 4-Year Degrees," *New York Times*, May 3, 2009, p. 23.

135 Narrative on Stafford, PLUS loans is from *FastWeb! College Gold*, Op. Cit., p. 82.

Chapter 9

141 Narrative on credit card legislation is from http://www.wisebread.com/ how-will-the-new-credit-card-rules-affect-consumers and from http:// money.cnn.com/2009/05/19/news/economy/credit_cards/index.htm.

141 Narrative on student survey on credits is from Kathy Chu, "Credit Cards Go After College Students: Banks Increase Efforts to Forge Relationships with Attractive Demographic," *USA Today*, March 31, 2008.

142 *BusinessWeek* research narrative is from Jessica Silver-Greenberg and Ben Elgin, "The College Credit-Card Hustle," *BusinessWeek*, July 28, 2008, p. 38.

142 Sears narrative is from Joe Hallinan and Amy Merric, "Credit Cards Swipe Sears Profiits," Wall Street Journal, Feb. 11, 2003, p. C.

143 Thirty-Five million pay the minimum balance narrative is from Robin Stein, "The Ascendancy of the Credit Card Industry," *Frontline*, November 23, 2004, http://www.pbs.org/wgbh/frontline/shows/credit/.

143 Per Canadian household narrative is from Paul Wallace, "Sound Canada, the envy of the U.S," Paul Wallace, *Euroweek*, September 17, 2009, p. 2.

143 Pay off balances narrative every month is from Trichur, Rita and Flavelle, Dana. "Fight to Cap Credit Card Interest Rates, Fees Heats Up." Toronto Star 24 Jan 2009 P. B 01. http://pqasb.pqarchiver.com/thestar/access/

144 Citibank, Delaware narrative is from *Frontline*, Op. Cit., p. 77.

144 In 2001 narrative is from "Ask Court Not to Block California Minimum Payment Disclosure Law," *Consumer Action*, October 24, 2002, http://www.consumer-action.org/archive/English/alerts/2002_10_24_AT.php.

144 In May of that year narrative is from Todd Davenport, "California Law on Card Warnings Struck Down," *American Banker*, December 26, 2002, p. 1.

144 Feinstein narrative is from David Lazarus, "Credit Card Debt Has Its Price," *Los Angeles Times*, January 30, 2008, p. C1.

144 Akaka narrative is from "Credit Card Minimum Payment Warning Act Introduced in Senate by Sen. Akaka," U.S. Fed News Service, April 24, 2007.

145 Richard Shelby narrative is from ibid. and "Politicians & Elections." Campaign Finance/Money Summary 2008. The Center for Responsive Politics. http://www.opensecrets.org/politicians/summary.php?cid=N00009220&cycle=2008.

145 Value of Homes and Live Richly narrative is from Louise Story, "Home Equity Frenzy Was a Bank Ad Come True," *The New York Times*, August 15, 2008, p. A1, C7.

145 Past due narrative is from ibid.

146 Highest levels ever recorded narrative is from Nancy Trejos, "Loan Delinquencies Hit Record High Last Year; Job Losses Hurt Consumers' Ability to Pay," *The Washington Post*, January 8, 2009, p. D3.

146 Overpriced California narrative is from Author Unknown, "California is industry's worst crash site," *Automotive News*, May 4, 2009, p. 42.

146 Since 2005 narrative is from Author Unknown, "Call Them Irresponsible," *The Wall Street Journal*, March 2, 2009, p. A14.

146 Americans' average equity rate narrative is from Alan J. Heavens, "Americans' Home Equity Lowest Since 1945," *Philadelphia Inquirer*, March 7, 2008.

146 According to a 2003 survey is from Danielle DiMartino, "Mortgage refinancings can hurt homeowners," *Dallas Morning News*, January 6, 2003.

147 Eager to pay off debt narrative is from Author Unknown, "Canadians, Eager to Pay Off Debt, May be Wary of Equity Loans," *National Mortgage News*, March 19, 2007.

148 Edward Koop narrative is from http://profiles.nlm.nih.gov/QQ/Views/Exhibit/narrative/tobacco.html.

149 Minimum payment narrative and tables are from "Minimum Payments, Maximum Costs on Credit Cards," *FDIC Consumer News—Summer 2003*, September 15, 2003, Federal Deposit Insurance Corporation, http://www.fdic.gov/consumers/consumer/news/cnsum03/minmax.html.

Chapter 10

151 Washer-dryer quote is from Michael J. Silverstein and Neil Fiske, *Trading Up*, New York, Penguin Group, 2003, p. 4.

155 Forty-three percent of kids narrative is from Jeremy Manier and Rubin Miller, "More toddlers have own TVs, study finds; 20% of children under age 3 have a set in bedroom," *Chicago Tribune*, May 7, 2007, p. 3.

155 More than $500 billion, minivan narrative is from Kim Campbell and Kent Davis-Packard, "How Ads Get Kids to Say, I Want It!" *Christian Science Monitor*, September 18, 2000, p. 1.

158 Narrative on FICO score is from "Understanding Your FICO Score," Fair Isaac Corporation.

Chapter 11

167 Narrative on film with Dirksen's comments is from Bara Vaida, Eliza Newlin Carney, and Lisa Caruso, "Potholes on K Street," *National Journal*, March 25, 2006, p. 16-25.

168 Quotes from Joe Scarborough are from Joe Scarborough, *Rome Wasn't Burnt in a Day*, New York, HarperCollins, 2004, p. 87, 88.

168 Narrative on Dan Miller is from Larry Makinson, *Speaking Freely; Washington Insiders Talk About Money in Politics*, Center for Responsive Politics, 2003, p. 33.

169 Narrative on Tim Roemer is from ibid., p. 69.

171 Narrative on hearing before the Senate Governmental Affairs Committee is from Dana Milbank, "For Would-Be Lobbying Reformers, Money Habit Is Hard to Kick," *The Washington Post*, January 26, 2006, p. A06.

171 Narrative on Leadership PAC money is from http://www.opensecrets.org/pacs/industry.php?txt=Q03&cycle=2008.

171 Narrative on Scott Thomas is from Jeffrey H. Birnbaum, "Election Commissioner Is a Lonely Voice," *The Washington Post*, October 3, 2005, p. D01.

172 Kent Cooper quote is from ibid.

172 Open seats narrative is from http://www.msnbc.msn.com/id/15348258

172 K Street Project narrative is from "The K Street Shuffle," *St. Louis Post-Dispatch*, February 16, 2004.

172 They went after narrative is from ibid.

172 Narrative on number of lobbyists is from Center for Responsive Politics.

173 Public Citizen narrative is from "Congress's Deepening Shadow World," *The New York Times*, April 14, 2005, p. A26.

173 Narrative on Santos book is from *Do Members of Congress Reward Their Future Employers?* Op. Cit., p. 64.

174 Narrative on Mandarin Hotel is from Jeff Zeleny, "Obama's Vows on Donations Collide With Reality," *The New York Times*, June 19, 2009 p. 1.

174 Narrative on farm subsidies is from "The Corporate Welfare Congress," *The Wall Street Journal*, October 23, 2007, p. A18.

174 Narrative on tax rate from corporate income is from Andy Stern, *A Country That Works*, New York, Free Press, 2006, Kindle edition, locations 2450-55.

175 Narrative on Congressional pay, pensions is from http://usgovinfo. about.com/library/weekly/aa031200a.htm.

175 Narrative on average age is from http://www.msnbc.msn.com/id/ 15348258.

175 Narrative on Nancy Pelosi is from Dick Morris and Eileen McGann, *Fleeced*, Harper Collins e-books, locations 1583-89.

176 Even when members of Congress do show up narrative is from ibid., location 1636-40.

176 Congress approval rating narrative is from Lydia Saad, "Congressional Approval Hits Record-Low 14%," The Gallup Poll Briefing, July 2008, p. 70.21

176 Bill Jefferson indicted narrative is from Matt Kelley, "Bribery trail begins today for Democrat," USA Today, June 9, 2009. p. A5.

176 Found guilty narrative is from http://www.khou.com/news/local/politics/stories/khou090806_tnt_jefferson-found-guilty.b2ee4312html

176 Randy Cunningham narrative is from, Paul von Zielbauer, "Ex-Lawmaker Is Unhelpful in Brice Case, Official Says," The New York Times, May 11, 2006, p. A32.

Chapter 12

179 Dodd narrative is from http://washingtontimes.com/news/2009/mar/30/aig-chiefs-pressed-to-donate-to-dodd.

179 Creation of PACs narrative is from Dan Clawson, Alan Neustadtl, and Denise Scott, Dollars and Votes, 1st ed., Philadelphia, Temple University Press, 1998, p. 13.

179 Explicitly political narrative is from National Journal, October 2002, Op. Cit.

180 Goldie-Morrison narrative is from Carrick Mollenkamp, "Bank of America Faces Allegations; Former Executive Charges Use of 'Creative' Accounts, Pressure for Contributions," The Wall Street Journal, November 12, 2003, p. C15.

180 CFO narrative is from Tim Reason and Don Durfee, "Office Politics," CFO, July 2004, p. 54-60.

181 Morgan Stanley narrative is from Caren Chesler, "Buttonholed! Are Wall Street Employees Pressured by Bosses to Give?" Wall Street Life, February 9, 2004.

181 According to Casey narrative is from "Greg Casey Talks About a New Program That Aims to Increase the Clout of Business in Politics," *Business News, New Jersey*, Vol. 14, Issue 41, October 9, 2001, p. 23.

181 Whereas 19% narrative is from Louis Jacobson, "Fighting the Political 'Ground War,'" *National Journal*, Vol. 34, Issue 41, October 12, 2002, p. 2983-2985.

182 Prosperity Project narrative is from Jonathan Rauch, "On the Web, Business Finds a New Way of Doing Politics," *National Journal*, Vol. 37, Issue 44, October 29, 2005, p. 3342-3343.

182 Under the program narrative is from ibid.

182 Casey quote is from ibid.

183 Employee Free Choice Act narrative is from Hart Research Associates Press Release, "Public Opinion Regarding the Employee Free Choice Act, National Survey Results," January 8, 2009.

184 Lincoln and Specter quotes are from Melanie Trottman and Brody Mullins, "Labor Bill Faces Threat in Senate," *The Wall Street Journal*, Mach 10, 2009, p. A1.

184 National Association of Manufacturers narrative is from http://www.bipac.net/page.asp?g=nam&content=homepage and http://www.bipac.net/issue_alert.asp?g=nam&issue=Paycheck_Fairness &parent=Nam.

185 International Association of Machinists and Aerospace Workers narrative is from *Wall Street Life*, Op. Cit.

185 Enron narrative is from Evan Thomas and Andrew Murr, "The Gambler Who Blew It All," *Newsweek*, February 4, 2002.

185 Outback narrative is from Jennifer Liberto and Aaron Rothenburger, "Rough Cuts," *Mother Jones*, November/December 1998.

Conclusion

192 Deductible IRA narrative is from *EBRI Notes*, May 2008, Vol. 29, No. 5, p. 7.

193 W. Edwards Deming quote is from W. Edwards Deming, *The New Economics*, Cambridge, MA, the MIT Press, 1994.

194 Andy Stern quote is from Andy Stern, "A Country that Works," Kindle Edition location 330, Op. Cit.

194 Fareed Zakaria narrative is from Zakaria, Fareed, "The Post-American World," Kindle Edition location 609.

194 Economic nationalism narrative is from Jeffrey E. Garten, "The Dangers of Turning Inward," *The Wall Street Journal*, February 28-March 1, 2009, p. W1.

194 Pew Global Attitudes narrative is from Zakaria, Op. Cit., location 624.

195 Smoot-Hawley narrative is from John Steele Gordon, *The Great Game*, New York, Simon & Schuster, 1999, p. 235.

195 A little-noticed provision narrative is from John D. McKinnon, "Banks Face Hurdles to Foreign Hires," *The Wall Street Journal*, February 21-22, 2009.

196 Canada has no such limits narrative is from Fareed Zakaria, "Worthwhile Canadian Initiative," *Newsweek*, February 16, 2009.

196 Companies are noticing narrative is from ibid.

196 Beacon of entrepreneurialism narrative is from "The United States of Entrepreneurs," *The Economist*, March 14, 2009, p. 9-13.

197 Immigrants account for narrative is from "The Post-American World," Op. Cit., location 2513.

197 A quarter of America's narrative is from "The United States of Entrepreneurs," *The Economist*, March 14, 2009, p. 9-13.

198   Innovation Hub narrative is from John Kao, *Innovation Nation*, New York, Free Press, 2007, p. 195-198.

198   Narrative on nanomolecular materials is from "Nanomolecular Science at Jacobs University," *SES-GA-Handbook-NANO*, p. 1.

198   Standardized test narrative is from National Center on Education and the Economy, *Tough Choices or Tough Times* John Wiley & Sons, 2007, p. xxi.

199   Recruiting smarter teachers narrative is from ibid., p. xxiv.

199   Japanese teachers' pay narrative is from *Thinking for a Living*, Op. Cit., p. 23.

199   In a speech narrative is from http://www.nytimes.com/2009/03/10/us/politics/10text-obama.html?_r=1

200   Arne Duncan narrative is from http://www.cnn.com/2009/POLITICS/02/27/education.school.year/index.html.

200   Preschool narrative is from John Mooney, "Aid Critical to Public Preschool Plan," *The New York Times*, March 1, 2009, p. 1.

201   Narrative on inflation rates in the 1970s and 1980s from Stocks, Bonds, Bills and Inflation 2007 Yearbook Morningstar, 2007, pp 36-37.

203   Many black leaders narrative is from "Black Leaders Torn Over Endorsement: For Many the Focus is on Electability," Shailagh Murray, *The Washington Post*, December 1, 2007, p. A6.

204   Want to win quote is from Dan Balz and Anne E. Kornblut, "Obama Joins Race with Goals Set High," *The Washington Post*, February 11, 2007, p. A1.

Index

FT Press

FINANCIAL TIMES

In an increasingly competitive world, it is quality
of thinking that gives an edge—an idea that opens new
doors, a technique that solves a problem, or an insight
that simply helps make sense of it all.

We work with leading authors in the various arenas
of business and finance to bring cutting-edge thinking
and best-learning practices to a global market.

It is our goal to create world-class print publications
and electronic products that give readers
knowledge and understanding that can then be
applied, whether studying or at work.

To find out more about our business
products, you can visit us at www.ftpress.com.